To Mary Yoko
My dear INSEAD
colleague

Cordialement

Laurence

Advance praise for *Build, Borrow, or Buy*

"*Build, Borrow, or Buy* provides an innovative and practical framework that will facilitate objective decision making, and as a result will help build a more disciplined path to growth."
—Arnaud Bernaert, Senior Vice President,
Corporate Mergers & Acquisitions, Philips Healthcare

"Choosing to build, borrow, or buy is a dilemma that every CEO has to face. This book provides CEOs with a simple yet powerful framework for making those decisions without making costly mistakes."
—Sucheth Davuluri, CEO, Neuland Laboratories Limited

"An insightful framework for thinking about one of the important strategic issues in today's increasingly complex and interconnected business world. Capron and Mitchell provide clear guidance on how to choose between internal development, licensing alliances, and M&A to select the most appropriate path to growth."
—Franz B. Humer, Chairman, Roche Group and Diageo PLC

"*Build, Borrow, or Buy* tackles the most difficult strategic decision facing companies in search of growth today. It is a well-balanced and clear analysis that should be required reading for every CEO."
—Kevin P. Ryan, Founder and CEO, Gilt Groupe

BUILD, BORROW, OR BUY

BUILD BORROW OR BUY

SOLVING THE GROWTH DILEMMA

LAURENCE CAPRON
WILL MITCHELL

HARVARD BUSINESS REVIEW PRESS

Boston, Massachusetts

Library of Congress Cataloging-in-Publication Data

Capron, Laurence.
    Build, borrow, or buy : solving the growth dilemma / Laurence Capron and Will
Mitchell.
        p. cm.
    ISBN 978-1-4221-4371-1 (alk. paper)
    1. Business enterprise—Finance.   2. Strategic planning.   3. Decision making.
4. Success in business.   I. Mitchell, Will. II. Title.
    HG4026.C247 2012
    658.4'012—dc23

                                                                    2012010778

Contents

Preface

In many ways, this book started at the University of Michigan in Ann Arbor during the fall of 1993. Separately, we were studying how firms sometimes survive and adjust within dynamic environments, particularly how firms use acquisitions, alliances, and other mechanisms to acquire and recombine strategic resources. Our first encounter and subsequent joint work led to two decades of close friendship between our families and to collaborative research and teaching on how firms compete and survive by developing sound resource-selection and resource-management strategies.

This book derives most directly from research we have done over the past decade—building on our earlier projects—into how firms "build, borrow, or buy" the resources they need to compete successfully and, specifically, how they choose from among the several sourcing options available to them. In the course of that research, we have been privileged to gain access to executives at some of the world's great businesses, across many industries and geographies. We are enormously grateful for the executives' willingness to share with us their experiences, good and bad. Their candor was inspiring, and their insights were indispensable to our progress. Their stories are peppered throughout the book.

We also have benefited greatly from the thinking and writings of colleagues and other scholars, who have provided key insights within the broad realm of evolutionary and ecological theories, dynamic capabilities, and interfirm exchange. We are particularly grateful for inspiration from Rajshree Agarwal, Erin Anderson, Ashish Arora, Jay

Barney, Glenn Carroll, Wes Cohen, Karel Cool, Michael Cusumano, Yves Doz, Kathleen Eisenhardt, John Freeman, Alfonso Gambardella, Philippe Haspeslagh, Bruce Kogut, Dan Levinthal, Marvin Lieberman, Phanish Puranam, Brian Silverman, Harbir Singh, David Teece, Michael Tushman, Oliver Williamson, Sidney Winter, and Maurizio Zollo.

Over the years, we have been fortunate to work on papers, articles, and case studies with talented coauthors who have helped us develop and deepen our thinking on firms' build-borrow-buy strategies. They include Gautam Ahuja, Jay Anand, Asli Arikan, Joel Baum, Rich Bettis, Fares Boulos, Nir Brueller, Olivier Chatain, Pierre Dussauge, Bernard Garrette, Mauro Guillén, Connie Helfat, Rebecca Henderson, Glenn Hoetker, John Hulland, Jung-Chin Shen, Kevin Kaiser, Samina Karim, Ishtiaq Mahmood, Xavier Martin, Anita McGahan, Louis Mulotte, Anuradha Nagarajan, Joanne Oxley, Anne Parmigiani, Urs Peyer, Nathalie Pistre, Karen Schnatterly, Myles Shaver, Kulwant Singh, Anand Swaminathan, Bart Vanneste, and Charles Williams. Their work, as well as other colleagues' work, is referenced in the appendices of this book.

We are equally grateful for all that we have learned from our students—in the various MBA, executive MBA, executive education, health management, and PhD programs at schools where we have taught and done research over the past twenty years. Given the diverse institutions at which we've had the pleasure of working (including University of California at Berkeley, Duke, HEC Paris, INSEAD, Ivey Business School, Kellogg, Michigan, MIT Sloan, Toronto, Wharton, University of Witwatersrand, and National University of Singapore), we have met legions of gifted students with impressively varied backgrounds, ideas, and outlooks. Their perspectives have made our book all the richer.

We have received outstanding encouragement and advice from our publisher and editors. David Champion helped us shape our ideas into an outline and then provided determined guidance as the book developed. Tamzin Mitchell and Matt Darnell provided early-stage editorial work that kept us from being too obscure. Lew McCreary pushed us with unflagging patience and equally unflagging stubbornness to clarify our logic, and then actually made the book readable. Melinda Merino was willing to take a chance on the book at Harvard Business Review Press.

Finally, we are profoundly indebted to our families. We could not have written this book without their amazing support and patience. Laurence is deeply grateful for the support of her husband, Pierre Chandon, and their three daughters, Louise, Claire, and Marie. Will is deeply grateful for the support of Dilys Bowman and their three children, Mairi, Tamzin, and Luc—and he promises to be home in an hour.

Laurence Capron
William Mitchell

Introduction
Two Funerals and a Wedding

There is something broken in the way many businesses obtain the resources they need to grow. Most companies are very good at identifying what those new resources are, and nearly all of them take that challenge seriously. And yet we have seen company after company—even highly regarded ones—get into trouble as they grow, because they paid much less attention to the right way to obtain resources than to the task of identifying them. Companies have underestimated the importance of making a well-considered decision about the right pathways to growth: whether to build, borrow, or buy. As a result, they go about choosing carelessly, without discipline, diligence, or guiding principles. Very often, in fact, they don't make a conscious choice at all; they do what they've always done, figuring that practice makes perfect. And later, when they have fallen short on a promising opportunity, they never suspect that the problem began with that long-ago careless choice.

Our aim in writing this book is to show you how to build a powerful new business capability: the discipline of selecting the best pathways to follow when pursuing growth opportunities. From our research, we have developed a comprehensive framework for deciding whether—under what sets of circumstances and in what combinations—to build, borrow, or buy your way to success. The three words that constitute the title of our book each express a point of view: (1)

build: *We'll do it ourselves*; (2) borrow: *We need others to help us*; and (3) buy: *We'll buy our way in.*

Of course, put like that, it sounds deceptively simple. But it's not.

Pursuing a new opportunity usually requires resources you don't yet possess. These might consist of some combination of skills, know-how, technologies, methods, broad competencies, and other assets. To compete for the opportunity, a company must either build the needed resources internally or obtain them from the outside.

Because decisions on how to obtain needed resources can seem straightforward, few businesses recognize how difficult—and how important—it is to choose wisely among even a limited number of options. Consequently, firms often choose reflexively, basing their decisions on familiar past practices and preferences after devoting little thought to the matter. As we will show, such heedless habits go a long way toward explaining why many viable strategies fail to live up to their potential.

To help explain the dilemma at the heart of our book, we offer three brief hypothetical cases. They show three businesses pursuing very different approaches to obtaining the resources they need to pursue significant growth opportunities. Let's call the strategies *path-dependent growth*, *opportunistic growth*, and *build-borrow-buy growth*. The first two scenarios sketch out the problem of poor path selection. The third points the way to the solutions we will describe in the coming chapters.

Path-Dependent Growth: The Plight of the One-Trick Pony

Merlin Manufacturing (all three examples are fictitious) is an engineering company with a track record of success in building industrial-control systems for customers in process industries such as oil refining and chemical manufacturing. Its products have typically been proprietary, highly complex, and heavily customized. Its traditional business model has been to work intensively, consulting with large industrial customers to produce tailored solutions.

Lately, however, customers have begun to demand Internet-based control systems capable of managing multiple manufacturing sites from a single location. Some executives at Merlin saw this coming, and there has been much internal debate over whether and when to add an Internet-based offering. However, many in the engineering group have been skeptical of the security and robustness of Internet process-control approaches. A wait-and-see consensus prevailed until one of Merlin's main competitors launched an Internet product line.

Over the years, Merlin had added to its technical capabilities mainly by acquisition. Like many companies that buy their way up the technology curve, Merlin believed it had become sophisticated in its ability to identify and acquire small, leading-edge upstarts and to absorb them successfully into its culture. Almost by default, the buy mode had become the company's weapon of choice in handling change in the industrial-control ecosystem. The company's growth strategy was path-dependent: in effect, Merlin had made itself a one-trick pony.

Over the years, Merlin had built tailored processes for acquisitions. It conducted regular mergers and acquisitions (M&A) training sessions presented by top business consultants and academics. Leadership increasingly emphasized acquisition excellence based on a highly evolved set of skills. The company believed its repeatable formula had become better and faster over time—as reflected in Merlin's rising stock price.

As had happened cyclically—with each new leap up the technology curve—Merlin now needed to ramp up its Internet process-control knowledge base. To enter this new market, Merlin would, of course, apply its magic acquisition formula and start making deals.

But Internet-based industrial control systems are a volatile new beast. Even Merlin's engineers viewed them with suspicion, and there was an uncharacteristic lack of internal understanding about how to evaluate potential targets and even what questions to ask. Nonetheless, Merlin forged ahead as best it could. But its deals in this new domain failed to produce the expected benefits. Due diligence was more difficult, negotiations were tougher, and integration was bumpy—with key people in the acquired businesses leaving even before the ink was dry.

Merlin quickly lost ground in the new business. Moreover, it suffered in its core areas as the new acquisitions siphoned off attention and investment. Merlin's stock price took a big hit, and executives scrambled to rebuild investor confidence—which proved to be more difficult than expected. Lacking its customary wizardry and now a takeover target itself, Merlin was bought and broken up by its archrival.

No matter which option a path-dependent firm reflexively favors, the company is likely to struggle with growth—especially in dynamic competitive situations. The path-dependent firm cannot respond effectively when its industry moves in new technical, market, or regulatory directions that both create new opportunities and trigger new threats to its traditional business.

Opportunistic Growth: When Arbitrary Choices Lead to Chaos

Maverick Publishing is an up-and-comer in the media industry. Its established competitors in traditional media face challenges from digital offerings that threaten the paper-based business model. Compared with these rivals, Maverick is highly driven, leaner, more agile, and now bursting with digital skills.

Where others engaged in timid gradualism and small experiments, Maverick was aggressive, taking every opportunity it could to obtain new digital resources. It listened to pitches from investment bankers and bought Internet media companies; it allied with partners that were developing interesting products in digital niches; it negotiated licenses for digital technical skills. It also gave internal development teams substantial latitude to create digital resources.

Maverick won kudos from media and business experts for its energetic strategy and for the way it mixed external partnerships with internal explorations—at a time when its competitors were much less exploratory, either internally or externally.

But even with Maverick's investments of money and time in amassing new resources, frustration had crept in among employees. The company was nowhere near as strong as it should have been in the market. Its acquired businesses were not well integrated, and no tangible synergies were emerging. No one had clear oversight of an increasingly apparent tangle of licensing and alliance partners. No one seemed able to articulate how each partnership should contribute to tangible offerings that would advance the digital strategy. The lack of clear and coherent direction demotivated employees, as many fragmented resource-development initiatives pulled people in different directions.

In its aggressive opportunism, Maverick acted quickly while others in the industry were overly cautious, vacillated, and wasted time. But it also acted arbitrarily. Too little strategic coordination guided its decisions as it funded some projects internally, worked with partners on others, and sought M&A targets for yet other projects. The firm struggled to exploit the potential benefits of all this activity. The result subjected employees to a chaotic process of expensive, time-consuming acquisitions and partnerships. Indeed, a reputation for extreme disorder came to characterize Maverick Publishing.

In contrast to one-trick Merlin, Maverick was partly on the right track in its use of multiple growth paths. But it failed to carefully analyze important circumstances and contingencies that, we have learned, must factor into decisions about which growth paths to choose for what kinds of resources. Instead, Maverick's decisions on whether to build, borrow, or buy were arbitrary in each instance. In this way, chaos was introduced into the DNA of Maverick's strategy.

Do you recognize similar tendencies in your own firm to fall prey to either path-dependent or opportunistic growth strategies? If so, what would constitute a more successful way of selecting the right pathways to growth?

Build-Borrow-Buy Growth: The Right Cure for Each Condition

Consider a third approach, the *build-borrow-buy* strategy. During the past thirty years, Panacea Pharmaceuticals has participated in the biotech revolution and led the creation of the evolving networked model of global innovation. Over time, the firm learned about new technologies and changing markets, relying increasingly on a mixed portfolio of internal R&D, basic contracts, alliances, and acquisitions to develop and market its pharmaceutical innovations.

The firm employs high-performing teams of internal R&D people throughout the world. But unlike some competitors, Panacea has long supplemented internal development with external sourcing. It has raised the bar high for investing in internal projects, most of which must draw upon the company's proven skills in core therapeutic areas.

Externally, the firm has resorted to multiple licenses, which give Panacea access to compounds, products, and targeted skills that complement internal activities. Panacea also pursued more complex partnerships—to jointly develop new products and explore new markets—when contracts were deemed insufficient to support high levels of partner interaction or to coordinate and protect key resources.

Wherever alliances led to steadily increasing strategic value or required more substantial collaboration, Panacea would try to convert them into acquisitions, buying out former partners. It also made direct acquisitions in strategically important therapeutic areas for which Panacea needed quick access to capabilities that would accelerate internal learning.

By carefully selecting different paths for obtaining new resources, Panacea underwent a radical transformation. It maintained its leading position as the industry expanded globally. It developed a disciplined understanding of when to build a new resource internally, when to contract or ally with other firms to borrow resources, and when to follow the demanding path of buying another company.

Unlike Maverick, Panacea learned how to properly mix build, borrow, and buy strategies. Unlike Merlin, it avoided relying on only one trick. Instead, Panacea has become multidexterous, a master of all three modes, with the seasoned judgment to know when each is warranted and most likely to produce success.

The Promise of the Book

Our research and experience suggest that a well-developed build-borrow-buy capability is a powerful tool for achieving growth. The book spells out a step-by-step resource pathways framework for choosing the best way of obtaining the resources you need to compete effectively when new opportunities arise. We call this creating a *strong selection capability*. (See "Glossary of Key Terms" at the end of this chapter for a rundown of terms we use throughout the book.)

As we elaborate on the resource pathways framework throughout the book, we will show how various large and small companies around the world developed sustainable growth strategies reflecting this framework. We will describe how some firms have grown faster, and with less disruption, than many competitors—becoming more profitable and developing long-term competitive advantages as a result. These firms avoid many of the perils of growth by applying a more orderly process, earning dividends from the hard work they invest in selecting and implementing their growth strategies. Conversely, we will show how companies that either fail to adopt or stray from these principles struggle to grow effectively. Indeed, such derelictions often contribute to the collapse of firms—whether they are taking their first steps after initial successes or are once-powerful industry leaders.

The ideas in our book may prove valuable for many decision makers: for CEOs and other members of the top management team who are shaping your firm's strategic vision, for members of corporate development staff who are identifying major steps for achieving the vision, and for any decision makers who help decide where and how to seek new resources. Each of these stakeholders has an indispensable leadership role in ensuring that the resource pathways framework will deliver powerful enterprise benefits.

We hope that you will benefit from this learning journey. To be sure, there is no foolproof, GPS-like system that provides a step-by-step guide to the resource pathways. Leaders must still exercise sound judgment and build organizations with the discipline to develop a strong selection capability. Only through the combination of wisdom and discipline can businesses achieve the optimal mix of build, borrow, and buy modes to pursue successful growth.

GLOSSARY OF KEY TERMS

The following terms will appear throughout the book:

- **Resources:** assets that a firm needs to create goods and services for customers; may include *physical assets* such as plants and equipment; *intangible assets* such as know-how and intellectual property; or *human resources*—employees and other internal and external stakeholders who contribute to your business activities.

- **Strategic resources:** resources necessary to reinforce current competitive advantages, to lay the groundwork for future advantage, or to do both.

- **Existing resources:** resources a firm currently owns or controls or to which it has established reliable access.

- **Targeted resources:** resources a firm currently lacks and wants for opportunities to create valuable new goods and services for existing and new customers.

- **Resource gap:** the distance between existing and targeted resources.

- **Selection capability:** a firm's ability to select the appropriate pathways to fill resource gaps.

- **Build—internal development:** changes that a firm undertakes on its own to create value by recombining existing capabilities or developing new ones. Such efforts may involve training internal staff, executing internal product development, hiring new staff, or building new plants. Internal development is the alternative to the three forms of external sourcing: borrowing via contracts, borrowing via alliances, and buying (acquisition).

- **Build—internal exploratory environment:** an independent space where teams—working either as Skunk Works or as formally chartered, independent units—can experiment with new ideas, resources, and business models. An exploratory approach can be valuable as a way of buying time to learn about uncertain opportunities.

- **Borrow—contract:** arm's-length agreements to buy existing products or services from third parties. Such arrangements include purchasing outright off-the-shelf technologies and services; in- or out-licensing the use of specialized knowledge sources, software, and services; basic market agreements; and consulting contracts.

- **Borrow—alliance:** ongoing collaborative partnerships with other firms or institutions (e.g., a university). In an alliance, two or more partners agree to commit resources to work together for a period while retaining strategic autonomy. Examples include equity and nonequity joint ventures, R&D and marketing alliances, corporate venture capital investments, multiparty consortia, franchises, and detailed outsourcing agreements. Alliances may involve relatively simple agreements or far more complex relationships, including multistage contracts, cross-investments, and complicated rights agreements. All forms of alliances involve ongoing interactions between independent actors that commit money and effort to sustain work over the duration of the agreement. The partners' independence means that they each have strategic autonomy; one firm cannot force its partners to do something.Alliances typically are guided by formal contracts, but all contracts are inevitably incomplete in the sense that they cannot fully specify all possible future events.

- **Buy—acquisition:** cases in which a firm purchases at least a controlling interest in another firm to obtain unfettered use of its resources. Acquisitions provide unified strategic direction for both the buyer and the target firm. Buyers sometimes continue to operate a target firm as an independent entity, at least initially, but have the right to integrate people and other resources across the two firms to combine operations and cocreate new resources. Acquisition might mean purchasing entire firms or individual business units from multi-unit corporations.

- **Divestiture:** the sale of business units, product lines, and major assets.

The Resource Pathways Framework

Business ecosystems change constantly. Opportunities come and go quickly. The race is won by those most agile and swift. To compete and grow, companies worldwide must regularly expand or reinvent their resources. Media businesses need new digital offerings, retail banks must add Internet banking services, automakers face pressure to offer green technologies, food companies' customers demand more-healthful products, and pharmaceutical firms need to constantly absorb the fruits of biomedical research. Indeed, there is hardly a sector in which change is not a permanent wild card.

The pace of this market-driven, technological, regulatory, and competitive ferment requires that companies continuously analyze and address the gaps in their existing knowledge and skills. Inevitably, these gaps present leaders with important choices.

Closing those gaps is an unending business challenge. Companies face a dizzying diversity of expert skills and knowledge sources and the growing global competition to acquire them. This competition spans both the developed world and the fast-growing emerging markets. More and more, firms find themselves navigating a global expanse of evolving geopolitical and institutional boundaries, a reality that affects new entrepreneurial businesses and deep-pocketed, established companies alike.

But no matter their size or pedigree, firms seeking to bridge resource gaps have a limited number of options: they can innovate internally (build); enter into contracts or alliances and joint ventures (borrow); or merge or acquire (buy). This trio of straightforward categories masks a complex mix of considerations that make selection difficult and outcomes uncertain. Articles in the business press highlight businesses' frequent failure to innovate successfully, to sign contracts or forge alliances that remain harmonious and productive, or to realize the predicted synergies of a seemingly potent acquisition.

Our research and experience have found that companies of all kinds across the globe struggle to find and manage the resources critical for their future success. Failure to obtain new resources has two root causes. First, and most visibly, firms often struggle to implement the paths they have chosen for obtaining resources; second, and less well understood, the paths chosen are often the wrong ones.

Because each path presents many difficulties, executives must understand when one path makes more sense than another. Indeed, choosing a wrong path will, in itself, make implementation more difficult and can lead to the *implementation trap*. In this trap, the firm fails because it tries harder and harder to implement the wrong way of obtaining key resources.

Our core message throughout this book is simple: *firms that learn to select the right pathways to obtain new resources gain competitive advantages.* Conversely, firms that do not carefully weigh competing paths, but instead dutifully replicate a preferred past method—no matter how diligently they pursue it—will often stumble and fail. They will lose ground to firms that pursue more disciplined approaches of reviewing, selecting, and balancing the different resource-development paths. ("A Tale of Two Deals" highlights the advantages and disadvantages of various pathways.)

As noted in the introduction, our step-by-step resource pathways framework helps you choose the best way of obtaining the resources you need to exploit strategic opportunities. Part of the framework's

A TALE OF TWO DEALS

Selection Mistake Meets Selection Success

The 2002 purchase of the Compaq Computer Corporation by Hewlett-Packard (HP) embodies a tale of two selection processes—one successful and the other not.

At the time of the $25 billion deal, HP's acquisition of Compaq was highly controversial. Yet, despite many predictions of catastrophe, the deal helped HP complete its transformation from a scientific instruments company into a personal-computing leader.

Less successful was an earlier pair of acquisitions by Compaq. From its founding in 1982 through the 1990s, Compaq grew to become one of the world's leading business and retail PC manufacturers. But in the mid-1990s, the company faced competitive pressure from Dell and other industry rivals. In 1997 and 1998, Compaq purchased Tandem Computers, a producer of high-end business computers, and Digital Equipment Corporation (DEC), a leading maker of minicomputers. Compaq believed that these two acquisitions would allow it to compete with the likes of IBM as a broad-based computer manufacturer.

But Compaq had no blueprint for integrating and exploiting the acquired properties. Fundamentally, it could not assess the feasibility of postacquisition integration or identify the right ways to fill complementary resource gaps. Compaq struggled to make the pieces fit together. The resulting fragmentation damaged its ability to compete successfully with better-integrated computer makers.

Compaq made two mistakes in its acquisition decision. First, it did not carefully assess the difficulties of absorbing two ambitious—and very different—acquisitions in consecutive years. Second, having failed to weigh integration issues, it had effectively overlooked potential problems that might have led it to walk away from the deal. Deals sometimes fall through, often for good reasons. If you are well informed enough to dodge a bullet, you then have the chance to shift gears and pursue a more appropriate business-transformation strategy. But Compaq was unable to recover from the failed acquisitions. It became available as a target.

Conversely, in the 1990s, HP had grown from its roots as a scientific instruments innovator, becoming a strong player in the minicomputer segment and an industry leader in PC printers. In the late 1990s, HP decided to focus on the computer industry. It separated its traditional scientific instruments unit and several related businesses into a separate company called Agilent. In 2002, HP saw Compaq as a lever to help expand its computer industry presence.

Unlike Compaq, HP paid considerable attention to how it would select the necessary resources for this strategy. It looked carefully at the feasibility of postacquisition integration and at ways of complementing the acquisition with both internal development and alliance support. Before completing the Compaq deal, HP set up a brigade of integration teams to specify activities the company would need to undertake to integrate Compaq's resources and to identify HP resources that would become redundant once the firms combined. The integration was led by a highly respected senior executive who reported directly to HP's CEO, Carly Fiorina. Immediately after the deal was completed, a senior executive from Compaq joined the integration team as coleader.

In parallel, HP's senior leadership recognized complementary resource gaps that the company would need to fill through build and borrow strategies. HP therefore set up multiple project teams to develop software and hardware bridges that would interconnect key parts of the newly integrated businesses (for example, linking Compaq's computers to HP's printer product lines). In addition, HP identified partners to help it expand the integrated business—for example, working closely with SAP to develop software HP would need for its expanded business-oriented services.

The combination of build, borrow, and buy strategies following the Compaq acquisition led to major changes at HP over the next decade—and ultimately to financial success. The company laid off thousands of people from the target companies and traditional HP units. At the same time, though, it added staff to support the change in strategic direction. The company quickly became the world's largest PC maker and reinforced its leadership in the printer business.

Early financial results were mediocre. There were losses in 2002 and low profitability through 2005. By 2006, however, the transformation had produced substantial success. The company had returned to strong profitability, growing sales by 50 percent while increasing staffing by only 10 percent.

Over the next five years, HP grew sales by a further 50 percent while the company maintained profitability—despite having doubled personnel as it invested in areas of the transformed business to build on its market leadership.

Of course, no single transformation can respond to ongoing competitive dynamics. In 2012, under new leadership, HP is considering new changes to the business mix. As part of this shift, the company acquired Autonomy Corporation for $10 billion in 2011, to provide resources that HP will need for expanding its enterprise information management business.

power is its simplicity. Even so, you can expect internal and external pressures to lead you and other decision makers on bumpy detours.

Why? It is human nature for business leaders to rely repeatedly on what they know best. Over time, organizations develop a dominant way of obtaining resources. A strong R&D business may naturally default to building through internal innovation; a business that has grown through acquisitions is likely to look at each new gap as an opportunity to buy again; and a company that values rapid response and high flexibility in new markets may prefer borrowing through expedient temporary alliances or well-defined contract purchases. Each kind of organization has grown into a default approach for getting what it needs. And each default approach has become the hammer to which every opportunity looks like a nail.

Consequently, most businesses will need to break old habits. And old habits die hard! You will need great discipline to stay the course. But if you do, you will respond to each new opportunity appropriately. Success will depend less on outside forces, such as markets and technologies, than on the discipline and commitment of key decision makers within the firm.

Most businesses think far too little about the pathway they select; instead, they focus on implementation—and end up wondering why all their hard work is unavailing. By focusing on the selection challenge, the resource pathways framework leads to more effective implementation, because of its emphasis on the right path. Let's start by comparing the basic pathway choices.

The Resource Pathways Choices

Building through internal development or innovation can create powerful new value by recombining a firm's existing resources, but even the most aggressive R&D firms can't create all the skills and resources they need solely through internal development efforts. Companies must draw on external sources to complement organic growth. External sourcing can take many forms. At the simplest level, a resource-seeking firm can contract with other organizations that are willing to sell the needed resources. Alternatively, it may acquire resources by collaborating with or purchasing another company.

Acquisition is often touted as the fastest way to obtain a portfolio of resources—along with supporting teams, processes, and cultures. Yet purchasing a business requires an arduous M&A transaction and the postmerger integration of the acquisition into the organization—a difficult process that often fails.

Although internal development and M&A are dramatically different paths, both allow the resource-seeking firm to exercise strong control over the needed resources and the value the resources ultimately produce. Since many firms assume that ownership or control of resources is necessary to achieve competitive advantage, they see themselves facing a simple choice to either build or buy.

That is a mistake. Borrowing new resources, through contracts or alliances with partner organizations, is often a valuable path. Contracts and alliances offer temporary access to targeted resources under more flexible terms and at lower risks and costs than other modes. As described below, this was certainly the experience of the pharmaceutical industry.

From Fortresses to Networks

Until the 1970s, the multinational companies in the pharmaceutical sector emphasized in-house R&D, production, and marketing resources. Companies relied mainly on organic growth, missing out on contributions from external innovators. During the subsequent decades, developments in biotechnology and genomics—amplified by the global spread of innovative resources—prompted many pharmas to open up their R&D processes to accommodate a mix of contracts, alliances, and acquisitions. Today, major pharmaceutical firms around the world—such as Eli Lilly (US), Sanofi-Aventis (France), Teva (Israel), and Astellas (Japan)—commonly pursue innovation and research as much outside as inside their own laboratories.

Thus, pharmaceutical firms are transforming themselves from the old self-contained, fully integrated model into a far more open and flexible networked model. In response to this new openness, a profusion of resource providers has emerged to serve the pharmaceuticals' growing appetite for knowledge assets and development tools.

This transformation is not unique to the pharmaceutical sector. Information technology is fueling a boom in firms specializing in knowledge development and aggregation and analytics. No matter the industry, the ability to obtain resources in different ways requires that you learn and master when to build, buy, or borrow resources.

All three major approaches to growth—build, borrow, and buy—are vitally important. Internal development projects, contracts, alliances, and M&A constitute tens of thousands of deals worldwide each year. Moreover, the growth in each type of activity involves nearly all industries and countries—with ever-greater volumes of cross-industry and cross-border investment and deals.

In all this activity, there is no discernible global shift from one dominant form of obtaining new resources to another. Instead, businesses increasingly require a sophisticated, enterprise-wide ability to use multiple modes of obtaining targeted resources *as circumstances warrant.*

Beating Different Paths to the Same Place

The choice of a path is neither obvious nor easy, but is unique to a particular company. Therefore, two companies from the same industry, facing similar competitive forces, might select different paths to obtain new resources. Assuming their choices were made by a careful consideration of multiple options, both paths could be right for those companies. Conversely, if each firm reflexively chose its traditional preference, the choice would only be the right path by accident!

Companies in the smartphone industry employ a wide variety of pathways to market these multifeatured devices. While some firms' selections show signs of careful consideration—including a sophisticated recourse to multiple strategies for different elements of the same innovation—others seem more a matter of trial and error.

For example, Nokia initially used a borrow strategy, forming an alliance in 1998 with the UK software firm Psion (in conjunction with Ericsson and Motorola) to develop the Symbian operating system. To gain full control of Symbian, Nokia eventually bought the operating system from Psion in 2004. Research In Motion, meanwhile, has pursued a build strategy to make its successful BlackBerry line more smartphone-like. But the company has yet to demonstrate that it has the necessary resources for internal development alone. And HP resorted to a buy strategy for its ticket into the smartphone market. In 2009, it acquired Palm, maker of the Palm personal digital assistant (PDA) and developer of the webOS operating system, which HP planned to use in devices ranging from smartphones to PCs. Apple, meanwhile, followed a sophisticated build-borrow-buy strategy for its iPhone, taking the lead in designing the operating system, while pursuing and managing various technology licenses and alliances for other components and making a few key acquisitions. Google, joining the smartphone fray from its leading Internet position, has used both buy and borrow strategies. It acquired the mobile software firm Android in 2005 and then supported the platform through an industry consortium of hardware, software, and telecommunication companies, complemented with alliances with smartphone providers such as HTC and Samsung.

Traditional publishing firms have also followed divergent paths to fill digital resource gaps. Publishing e-books, online magazines, and other digital assets calls for skills both highly diverse and distinct from those of traditional publishing. Among them are the abilities to create multiplatform content, master data analytics, and interact with online communities.

To close its digital resource gaps, the Finnish media company Sanoma Group acquired a Dutch digital publishing company, Ilse Media, which then drove digital growth across the company. Axel Springer, the leading German publishing group, made significant internal investments in building the digital skills of its existing journalists and marketing people while creating integrated newsrooms and a cross-media advertising sales group.

Springer quickly discovered that it couldn't generate enough growth by turning traditional print into digital formats. So it changed paths and embarked on multiple acquisitions of "native" Internet businesses (AuFeminin.com and immonet.de) that were only indirectly related to core print activities. Springer has operated the acquired businesses on an arm's-length basis as it decides how best to integrate them over time. This example—like others whose first path chosen was eventually abandoned—shows how an ill-considered selection may produce disappointing results.

The British publisher Pearson Group pursued a mixed buy-build strategy, acquiring digital companies even as it sought to upgrade the skills of internal staff and to bridge the cultural divide between digital and print media. And the Associated Press entered into long-term partnerships with selected technology providers rather than acquire or develop internally the technical skills needed to create digital offerings.

In the automobile industry, similarly, manufacturers have adopted different ways of obtaining premium-market resources. Toyota has used internal growth to make inroads on the premium market with its

Lexus branded cars. Many other firms have used acquisitions to rapidly acquire premium technologies and brand names. The Indian conglomerate Tata bought Jaguar in 2008 from its US parent, Ford, and the Chinese car firm Geely acquired Volvo in 2010, also from Ford. Still other car firms have turned to contractual agreements: the Romanian automaker Dacia licensed technology from Renault (and later became part of the French firm). There are also more substantial partnerships, such as the multiproduct alliances between the French automaker Peugeot-Citroën and the Japanese automaker Mitsubishi Motors (on 4×4 and electric vehicles in 2005 and 2010, respectively) and the Franco-German equity joint venture formed in 2011, BMW Peugeot Citroën Electrification, to develop hybrid systems.

With all that choice, how do companies select the right path to obtain a specific resource that they need? Do they follow specific guiding principles? Do the principles depend on the nature of the gap, external pressures, internal skills and personnel, costs, the need to act quickly, the CEO's inclinations, or other factors? In reality, all these conditions are relevant when a company seeks strategic resources.

Given the stakes, you might expect that companies would have well-developed processes for selecting the best mode for acquiring new resources. But dysfunction is surprisingly more the norm than the exception. Our research over the years has shown that executives are often confused about the best way to obtain resources. They lack access to tools, guidelines, or even shared company wisdom that would help them make sound decisions. The following example—from a study we conducted in the global telecom industry—illustrates the consequences.

The Implementation Trap

In the late 1990s, a leading European supplier of telecom technologies, with a strong position in voice technology, launched an effort to compete in the fast-developing data environment. The company—well known for its superior engineering skills—had long favored internal R&D, so that was the path it chose. Because most data-networking innovation was then occurring in Silicon Valley, the company had difficulty competing for enough new talent to sustain the internal development effort. Lacking relevant know-how, the company failed in its internal innovation efforts.

Ultimately, the company's executives realized that they lacked not only the necessary technical skills but even the industry contacts and level of insight needed to identify best-of-breed technologies, consulting partners, and top talent. So they forged an alliance with an up-and-coming firm in Silicon Valley, hoping that the collaboration would help them quickly boost their market credibility and data networking skills. But the alliance lasted only a few months before disagreements between the partners over market and technology strategy caused a damaging bottleneck that undermined collaboration.

After these internal development and alliance activities failed, the company finally decided to acquire three US companies and combine them into a new US-based firm that would run the data communication business for the corporate group. The acquisitions finally gave the company a credible position in data networking.

An executive at this firm described the painful trial-and-error process, from building to borrowing to buying: "Each failure revealed more of this pattern: that we needed to reach a certain threshold of competency before we could run effective internal development or be an effective partner within an alliance. We had to finally turn to acquisitions in order to accelerate R&D."

The stories of this company and many others exemplify the *implementation trap*: a company works doggedly to perfect the wrong course of action. It plays out like this: faced with a need for new resources, a company pursues them in ways it believes worked in the past. For instance, R&D teams typically prefer to develop future capabilities through organic innovation. As one telecom executive told us: "We have superb technical skills on the engineering side. Internal people tend to think they should be given a chance to do it on their own. We need to break this perception barrier . . . We need to develop a capability to manage alliances and acquisitions. The issue is how you bring such process skills into our people's mind-set."

Unfortunately, when companies do try to break that barrier by trying something new, they tend not to stick with it long enough. An executive at a leading US telecom company shared with us his frustration that his company, instead of exploring the roots of its early failures with alliances, simply ruled them out of future consideration.

The result is that many firms adopt a small set of methods for managing their corporate development activities. Indeed, when adding to its strategic arsenal, the typical company relies heavily on just one dominant path—commonly either internal development or acquisitions— perhaps complemented with a supplemental method.

For instance, our study of the telecommunications industry found that only one-third of the surveyed firms actively used more than two methods of obtaining new resources. About 40 percent relied heavily on one main way of growing. When those companies did add a string to their bow, it was usually just one additional pathway: for example, M&A to complement internal development.

Reliance on only one dominant mode leads firms to believe that their success depends on working hard at implementing that mode. Business leaders often blame poor implementation when their firms struggle in the effort to add new resources. More than half of the 162 telecom firms we surveyed flagged implementation—particularly the lack of personnel and skills (67 percent) and an inability to integrate external resources effectively (50 percent)—as the primary cause of problems.

But the blame is misplaced. The real culprit is an ineffective process for selecting the right paths for obtaining resources. Sticking to a familiar or popular path may work in the short term. But in the long term, the implementation trap becomes a self-reinforcing cycle, with each new resource an occasion for continuously improving implementation of the wrong activities. To be sure, firms that fall into the trap do end up doing the wrong things quite well. They then become deeply frustrated when they struggle competitively. Assuming that the cause is implementation perpetuates the problem.

Instead, executives must think carefully about the important work that *precedes* implementation: the disciplined process of selecting the best way to obtain new resources. Firms that select the best path integrate new resources more quickly, cheaply, and effectively than do competitors. Our telecom study revealed that firms using multiple modes to obtain new resources were 46 percent more likely to survive over a five-year period than those using only alliances, 26 percent more likely than those using only M&A, and 12 percent more likely than those using only internal development.

Of course, some companies invest considerable time and effort in their build-borrow-buy decisions. Throughout the book, we will draw on many of the firms we have studied, including well-known companies from around the world. But even leading firms can make mistakes, sometimes rushing into deals without thoroughly exploring the implications, or succumbing to internal or external pressures to favor one pathway over another. The discouraging results of such lapses remind the firms to reassert the necessary discipline. Let's look now at what that discipline involves.

Finding Your Resource Pathways

The resource pathways framework allows you to compare the potential benefits and risks of all the possible sourcing modes and, ultimately, select the best option for obtaining needed resources. In devising the framework, we've assumed that your firm has developed its corporate strategy and identified its resource gaps—whether through structured planning activities or other more ad hoc processes. Nonetheless, the sidebar "Recognizing Resource Gaps" highlights problems that can arise if that work has not been done properly. As a useful preliminary, you may want to revisit initial strategic planning activities and confirm that identified resource gaps and targeted resources align well with your firm's broader strategy.

RECOGNIZING RESOURCE GAPS

The old adage about errant computer data—"garbage in, garbage out"—applies to the challenge of correctly identifying resource needs. It's unproductive to follow the right pathway to the wrong resources. Consequently, you need to make sure you target the right resources.

Companies sometimes stumble at the initial stage of targeting the right resources for the strategy they have set, especially when they have enjoyed great success in a dominant core domain. When it comes time to pursue a new strategy, with a new product line or in a new market, companies' past habits and expectations may lead them to misjudge the needed resources. Ingrained competencies, entrenched processes, and the power of existing brands can impede a clear-eyed assessment of resource gaps—particularly when the gaps result from disruptions in the competitive environment or from emerging fields or markets.

A prototypical example of this type of failure occurred when successful producers of steam locomotives responded to new diesel and electric locomotives by producing the most advanced, cost-competitive steam locomotives ever seen. Despite their hard work, these once-famous companies disappeared into the mists of business history, seen only thereafter on the logos of toy trains.

More recently, both Nokia and Research In Motion have struggled to respond to advances in consumer smartphones. Both companies overvalued the relevance of their existing internal resources in responding to advances from Apple, Google, HTC, and Samsung. Each has lagged badly in the smartphone market.

A form of myopia prevents companies from seeing that their existing core resources are unequal to the competitive demands of the moment—a problem caused by misaligned resource-management strategies. Consider what happens when management is properly aligned. In the locomotive example of the early twentieth century, a few steam locomotive producers—perhaps most notably Siemens—recognized the opportunity to build on their existing resource base by allying with firms possessing expertise in diesel and electric technologies. They became leaders in the new field because they targeted the right resources—the ones they lacked internally but recognized as core to their future survival. Likewise, in the smartphone market, Samsung combined internal development with focused alliances to take a leading position in Android-based systems.

New competitive realities often call for radically different resources. If your company fails to understand what resources it needs to compete in the future, it makes little difference what pathway you take to obtain them. If you have doubts about which resources your company needs to achieve its goals, your first step should be to use your company's strategic planning process to identify key resource gaps.

Assessing the Different Resource Pathways

The framework focuses on resources you deem to be strategically important—those that, when added, will either reinforce your existing competitive advantages or lay the groundwork for new ones. We will continue to stress the question of strategic importance, because it will help you think about how much to invest in resources that turn out to have less strategic value than you initially believed.

Four questions frame the selection of the different pathways (internal development, basic contracts, alliances, and acquisitions). These questions derived from our field interviews and work with firms across various industries and countries. We validated the relevance of the four criteria through a large-scale survey that we administered within the global telecommunications industry and through subsequent discussions with executives in many industries and countries and with our MBA and executive MBA students. Figure 1-1 illustrates the resource pathways framework as a decision tree addressing the four key questions.

Although the questions are general enough to address most contexts, we offer additional detail throughout the book to help you tailor your own decisions to your company's particular circumstances. The

FIGURE 1-1

The resource pathways framework as a decision tree

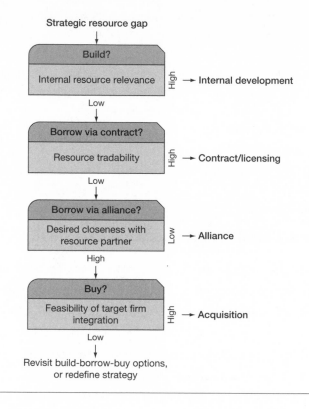

balance of this chapter summarizes the four key questions that will guide your path selection.

Question 1. Are Your Internal Resources Relevant?

Can you leverage existing company resources to satisfy new needs? Developing new resources internally is often faster and more effective than obtaining them from third parties. But this strategy is viable only when internal resources (knowledge bases, processes, and incentive systems) are similar to those you need to develop *and* superior to those of competitors in the targeted area. If so, your internal resources are relevant.

Often, existing resources will not be relevant. For instance, most traditional publishing firms' legacy print-media resources were so far removed from digital media that publishers had to bring in outside resources through acquisitions and partnerships—often after trying without success to have inside staff learn the ropes.

Likewise, a global investment bank recently sought to develop a private-equity business in Eastern Europe. The CEO of the country unit first assessed whether internal development might be feasible, but concluded that the local bank lacked sufficient expertise to develop a private-equity offering internally. Nor did the parent company have private-equity experience—which requires a deft understanding of activities ranging from deal origination to exit strategies. The CEO considered hiring away a competitor's team to support internal innovation. However, not only would that be expensive, but the bank would also risk being unable to retain and leverage the outside team's expertise. After concluding that internal resources lacked relevance for the new business, the CEO began reviewing external options.

You might think answering this first question is easy. Yet companies often vastly underestimate the actual distance between their existing resources and the targeted resources. Like many print publishers, business leaders more easily see the similarities than the profound differences: "Reporting, writing, and editing are the same for a Web page as a printed newspaper, right?" Well, yes and no. Traditional publishers failed to grasp radical shifts in the business model, technology, customer and revenue strategies, and the implications of community interaction—all of which continue to evolve. Seeing only what's similar, a business can fixate on internal development because it doesn't know what it doesn't know.

Internal development is fraught with obstacles that firms often overlook—until later. Businesses choose the build path as their first option and only consider external sources after encountering major setbacks. Among our sample of telecom firms, 75 percent used internal development as their preferred means of obtaining new resources. But when asked to evaluate the effectiveness of the internal path, many executives admitted they were disappointed. Almost half said that they failed to create the desired new resources because they were unable to properly manage internal development, and nearly two-thirds reported friction associated with integrating and diffusing the internally created resources throughout their organization.

In chapter 2 we will review how to assess the relevance of your existing resources for internal development and how to recognize—even at the outset of the selection process—when it is best to go straight to external sourcing.

Question 2. Are the Targeted Resources Tradable?

Once you've determined that you need to look externally for resources, you must weigh which type of external sourcing mode to use—from the simplest and most straightforward to those of higher cost, complexity, and commitment. (By tradable, we mean that you can negotiate and write a basic contract that will both protect the rights of the contracting parties and specify how they will exchange resources.)

The first option is obtaining what you need via contract, a basic form of borrowing resources that another firm has created. Arm's-length contracts often help companies identify, evaluate, and obtain bundles of new resources and absorb them quickly. Pharmaceutical firms commonly license the rights to register and market other companies' drugs in particular geographic markets. Chemical firms have long used contracts as a way of obtaining new molecular compounds. In turn, the companies sometimes out-license the rights to compounds or applications that they do not want to develop themselves. For example, W. L. Gore and Associates licenses the rights to use DuPont's PTFE polymer for use in medical implants and rain-resistant clothing. The two companies have always managed these relationships using basic contracts.

Contracting is often the simplest way of obtaining needed resources. However, companies often overlook it. Instead, they seek first to pursue an alliance or acquisition. We found that many firms overestimate their need for strategic control while underestimating the likelihood of achieving adequate control through third-party relationships. Overvaluing your need for control can lead you to paths that waste resources and, worse, deny you the opportunity to learn from independent partners. Yes, you need to protect your firm's core resources, but selecting the wrong sourcing mode can inhibit your ability to replenish that core.

Trust plays a role in answering this question. Firms often fear that an external party may not play fair in the agreements or that they may have to give up too much revenue to a contractual partner if they do not control commercialization. Only a third of the telecom firms we surveyed actively use contracts to obtain new resources. In fact, 70 percent said they would choose an alliance or acquisition over a contract, especially when the targeted resources affect core parts of their business. Only 30 percent of the surveyed firms had made systematic efforts to assess external resources available from suppliers. Thus, most firms decide on more complicated external sourcing options without first considering the simpler expedient of licensing through a basic contract. Such an oversight is often counterproductive.

It is important to carefully weigh potentially favorable conditions for a basic contract *before* turning to alliances and acquisitions—which require substantially greater management time and attention. Obtaining new resources via contract requires clarity in defining the targeted resources. Likewise, you must understand how the value of the new resources will be protected (and have some familiarity with, and confidence in, the relevant legal system).

Of course, sometimes a contract is inappropriate. But a company can't make that judgment without first investigating the option. Recall the global investment bank that wanted to launch a private-equity service through its Eastern European unit. Its leadership team initially weighed whether to contract with a local private-equity firm. In such an arrangement, the global business would provide products, brand equity, and global coordination while the local partner would provide local investment selection, deal structuring, monitoring, and exit skills. Such a contract would have required a solid incentive structure to secure strategic alignment with the partner. Alignment was critically important because the bank alone would have dealt with clients regarding investment results, processes, ethics, and partner due diligence. Moreover, the arrangement would require the private-equity firm to hire new employees to handle tasks that it did not explicitly contract to perform. After reviewing this option, the team concluded that the transaction costs between the two parties would be prohibitively high—driven up by the extensive coordination needs and by concerns that the partners might either take advantage of the relationship or fail to execute their responsibilities fully.

Chapter 3 will review how you can assess the tradability of your targeted resources. Tradability will help you decide when to obtain targeted resources via basic contracts, such as in-licenses and out-licenses, and when to consider more complex arrangements, such as alliances and acquisitions, with other firms.

Question 3. How Close Do You Need to Be with Your Resource Partner?

If your targeted resources are not easily tradable, you will need to consider an alliance or acquisition. Given a choice between those options, our message is simple: because M&A is the most complex path, reserve it only when it really pays to have a deep collaboration with the resource provider.

Alliances can take many forms, ranging from R&D and marketing partnerships to freestanding joint ventures. Thus, alliances might be relatively simple agreements or complex relationships involving multi-stage contracts, cross-investments, and complicated rights stipulations. All alliances, however, rely on ongoing interactions in which independent actors—these may be competitors, complementary firms, or other organizations (such as universities and public institutes)—commit resources to a joint activity.

Pharmaceutical companies commonly use alliances to develop and market specific drugs. In many cases, simply in-licensing the rights to a molecule would be risky because of the need to participate actively in the development process. Falling short of the intense control of an acquisition, alliances allow partner firms to collaborate on focused projects with explicit aims.

Of course, some projects are so complicated that the level of partner interaction renders the collaboration unworkable. In the Eastern European bank unit, for example, the alliance option at first seemed promising. It combined the strengths of global and local resources and strong incentives for the local partner to work hard to expand the business. The team rejected this option—after much consideration—because the bank's dominant motive in undertaking the strategy was to build a broad set of skills *for itself* and to keep tight control over the investment process. The bank concluded that the local private-equity partner would be loath to help launch a new competitor. Worse, the partner might use its close alignment to glean competitive insights for the future. There was also a secondary misgiving: most private-equity firms are unaccustomed to the stringent requirements of more traditional banks. The team feared that the structure of the joint venture would be likely to create ongoing conflicts between the partners about governance and processes.

Paranoia is a common business condition. Many firms are simply suspicious of collaboration, often for the wrong reasons. As we noted above, many executives overvalue control—and believe that collaboration will reduce their control over resources.

In our conversations with executives from telecommunication incumbents, many viewed alliances "as a route to diminishing our skills," as a way "of shopping core competencies rather than sharing knowledge," and as eventually transforming partners into competitors. Fully 80 percent of the surveyed executives shared concerns of exclusivity, control, and resource protection. Not surprisingly, 80 percent also reported that they used M&A, rather than alliances, to gain exclusive access to the firm controlling the needed resource. More than two-thirds of the executives also wanted to keep their own assets closely held, choosing M&A over alliances to protect their differentiation and unique resources.

As you can see, alliances are often tricky to manage. Some analysts suggest that no more than 30 percent of alliances succeed in meeting the partners' respective goals. Because alliances are almost always transient relationships, executives naturally fear the negative consequences of collaborating with a partner that might abuse them before or during the alliance or after exiting it. Those who can overcome such fears will have to actively manage alliances throughout their life cycles and easily foresee milestones and termination. Despite the risks, however, you should carefully assess the potential of an alliance before jumping heedlessly onto the acquisition path.

Chapter 4 will help you decide how to choose between alliances and acquisitions when interfirm collaboration is needed. As we will demonstrate, alliances are most effective when relatively few people and organizational units from each party must work together to coordinate the joint activities. A limited cast of characters also makes it easier to align the partners' incentives. But if the joint actions to obtain and develop strategic resources require *deep* involvement—for coordinating the use of resources or attempting to align goals, or both—you will usually benefit by considering an acquisition. You will have bought not only key resources, but also the assurance of retaining the value of their successful exploitation.

Question 4. Can You Integrate the Target Firm?

Before choosing the M&A path, bear in mind that acquisitions are almost always more time-consuming and expensive than even the most pessimistic scenario you could imagine. Acquisition is, for good reason, the mode of last resort—reserved for cases that don't suit any other path. However, that doesn't mean you must undertake an acquisition simply because you've analyzed and rejected the other modes.

If you value strategic control over the targeted resources and have already concluded that less integrative modes (contracts or alliances) will not achieve what you seek from the relationship, then you must assess whether you can effectively integrate the target firm's resources without damaging employee motivation *at either firm*. In our private-equity example, the team members were ultimately considering whether a skilled local target existed and was willing to sell at a viable price. They had concluded that acquisition appeared to be the optimal path. It offered the fastest way of developing a product. Unlike a team lift-out, in which a team is hired away from a competitor, an acquisition would bring the target's full pool of assets (including reputation) to the bank. The buy mode also offered greater freedom in restructuring local operations. Finally, the Eastern Europe unit would benefit from the support of its global parent, which has strong skills in pre-acquisition due diligence and postdeal integration of new personnel and assets.

However, the corporate development team was fully aware of the integration challenges and the importance of retaining the targeted resources. An acquisition would work only if the acquired resources could be fully leveraged to generate investment opportunities and strong investment performance. Moreover, the acquirer would have to provide value by bringing its expertise in legal, compliance, and risk management and by securing a solid country distribution base. In short, the team had to assess whether postdeal integration was feasible before deciding on acquisition.

It is very hard to make M&A succeed. For every successful story, there are multiple failures: some studies suggest that—as with alliances—just 30 percent of M&A achieve their goals. The main reason is that integrating the acquired entity almost always involves unanticipated obstacles and expenses. Personnel you wish to retain—because of their strong skills—typically have other opportunities, which they frequently pursue. The tremendous power and potential of the buy mode is matched by the severity of its challenges. For this reason, it is important to use acquisitions selectively.

Chapter 5 will help you decide under what circumstances to commit to an acquisition instead of other options that initially seemed infeasible. If you most likely cannot integrate the acquired target's resources within your organization, then you must reconsider the alternatives: set up more complex versions of the different sourcing modes and view them as learning experiments; explore the possibility of targeting substitute resources; or review your strategic goals and then revise or abandon the current resource search.

Managing the Portfolio

The framework we describe in this book not only applies to decisions concerning the acquisition of resources but can also help a firm dynamically manage how it owns and manages those acquired resources over time. In chapter 6, therefore, we present a model for continuously assessing existing resources, resource gaps, and needs for divestiture of resources that have outlived their usefulness. Finally, in chapter 7, we help you manage a balanced build-borrow-buy portfolio and develop a strong selection capability within your organization. These responsibilities require not only a rigorous approach to each sourcing decision, but also the ability to balance all such decisions across your organization, over time. In that way, you can maintain a viable combination of building on existing skills and exploring new opportunities. This balance clearly poses significant leadership challenges that we will highlight in our discussion.

Let's now look at the first choice that you need to make as you embark on the acquisition of a new resource.

When to Build

Internal Development Versus
External Sourcing

For good reasons, most businesses naturally think of internal development first when they need new resources. The search for strategic resources is ultimately about gaining a competitive edge. And resource ownership often goes hand in hand with competitive advantage. The ability to control intellectual property affords the greatest opportunity for ongoing profits—as long as you are the first to succeed with differentiated products. The more your firm can do on its own, the better able it should be to integrate, control, and protect core resources. And in the bargain, it will avoid the trouble and expense of finding, pricing, integrating, and recombining resources from third parties.

In our telecom study, 70 percent of the executives surveyed preferred internal development to external sourcing when they needed to develop differentiated products and services. An even higher 75 percent believed internal development would more effectively protect their firms' market differentiation and unique resources.

There is a further benefit to using internal development teams: it keeps them on their toes. They tend to maintain and enhance their skills and esprit de corps. Like any muscle, internal R&D stays toned through use. Otherwise, there is the risk of atrophy.

In research we conducted with auto sector suppliers, executives often reported they suffered from relying too heavily on external sourcing. The Romanian automaker Dacia manufactured licensed versions of French Renault models for more than thirty years before exiting the industry without ever having developed a single indigenous model (Renault acquired Dacia in 1999). Conversely, the Korean automaker Hyundai initially developed cars in collaboration with Ford, but ultimately absorbed enough internal expertise to design and successfully market its own models.

Without question, maintaining robust internal development capabilities is important. But sometimes, your in-house capabilities just aren't enough, and you must complement them with external resources. In this chapter, we will show how the resource pathways framework can help you identify circumstances where the use of internal resources is—and isn't—warranted.

Companies that build new resources internally naturally believe they have the necessary expertise. Internal development is most effective when existing resources—including your knowledge bases, processes, and incentive systems—relate closely to the new resources you need *and* outshine your competitors' in the targeted area. Your existing organization must also be compatible with the needed resources.

But you can have too much of a good thing. Businesses commonly misjudge the prospects for internal development by overestimating the relevance of their existing resource base. Many firms also pay scant attention to organizational fit (see the sidebar "Coca-Cola FEMSA Enters the Mexican Coffee-Vending Market"). No matter how hard firms work on implementation, they commonly fail if they use internal development in the wrong contexts.

COCA-COLA FEMSA ENTERS THE MEXICAN COFFEE-VENDING MARKET

The Challenge of Redeploying Internal Resources into New Uses

Coca-Cola FEMSA is the leading Latin American bottler of a wide variety of soft drinks. The Mexican company is 54 percent owned by Fomento Económico Mexicano S.A. de C.V. (FEMSA), 32 percent owned by The Coca-Cola Company, and 14 percent owned by public shareholders. Coca-Cola FEMSA is recognized for its innovative and robust distribution network—an industry benchmark known for its ability to adapt quickly to changes in the complex array of Latin American markets.

In 2010, the company sought to enter the coffee vending business as part of its growth path into new beverage categories. With Coca-Cola's successful launch of similar product portfolios worldwide, the Latin American bottler thought it could take advantage of these best practices in the soft-drink world. Coca-Cola FEMSA was particularly keen to challenge the leading position of Switzerland's Nestlé in Mexico's coffee vending business.

The venture project, enthusiastically championed by top management, received strong financial support. The company was determined to aggressively push the products to market and challenge Nestlé's dominant position. Nonetheless, the venture had a rough start and disappointing early results. Customers disliked the flavor of the new coffee product, named Blak. The distribution and maintenance of coffee vending machines was poorly executed. Moreover, significant internal tensions arose between people managing existing resources and the staff introducing Blak. As a result, Blak wasn't selling well.

The key problem was that the resource gap was much wider than initially thought. For Coca-Cola FEMSA, coffee vending was a brand-new category. It required a different knowledge base and different processes and organization. The skills and knowledge of the soft-drink business had little relevance to the coffee market. The new business suffered from the dominant soft-drink mindset of executive management.

Knowledge Fit

Across the value chain, Coca-Cola FEMSA applied knowledge and skills from the soft-drink business to the new coffee-vending market, most notably in product development and supply chain management. The company believed that the initiative fit closely with the company's existing internal resource base, which we refer to as high "knowledge fit" (we define knowledge fit in greater detail later in the chapter).

Assuming that product development would follow the same process as the cold soft-drink products business, the company started by making a coffee syrup. The syrup was to be mixed inside the vending machine with milk powder and the same water that was used for Coca-Cola. Once Coca-Cola released Blak, the team realized that the milk powder had a short shelf life, which in part explained customers' objections to the product's flavor. The product team had to retreat to the market-research stage and redevelop the beverage, eliminating the syrup (like Nestlé) to improve the flavors.

A second key challenge lay in distribution strategy and the supply chain. The coffee vending machines, placed next to soft-drink machines in small stores, were maintained like soft-drink machines. But what worked well for soft drinks was wrong for coffee. For example, the machines needed more frequent attention to make sure the milk powder didn't go bad. Worse, the newly designed machines often broke down and remained broken for long periods. And delivery-truck drivers—accustomed only to maintaining soft-drink machines— didn't know how to service the coffee machines and did not want to take the time to do so in any case. Finally, the warehouses lacked adequate space for the coffee product line; the new items interfered with regular loading processes and cycles, causing tension and confusion. Soon enough, the coffee products came to be seen as interlopers in the warehouses.

Organizational Fit

The initiative also suffered from organizational tensions, which we refer to as "organizational misfit" (we define organizational fit in greater detail later in the chapter). When Coca-Cola FEMSA launched Blak, the organization was optimized to handle soft-drink bottling, not "non-softs" like coffee. Truck drivers—who controlled the space in their trucks—were paid per box of goods delivered; sacrificing space reserved for sure-selling soft drinks to carry coffee supplies cut into their income. Moreover, coffee drivers needed different skills than those of traditional soft-drink drivers. The new group needed to clean the machines; restock them with coffee, milk, and sugar powders; and sell the coffee concept to retail store managers. Taken together, these duties required a different pay scale, which created conflicts with soft-drink handlers. Finally, at the executive level, the launch of Blak did not receive sufficient focused attention, which led to insufficient resources having been invested in strategic planning and research.

Coca-Cola FEMSA learned from its setbacks. In 2011, it relaunched as a pilot program in Mexico City. The company modified the product, upgraded internal resources, selectively obtained some external resources, and developed dedicated functions—including a separate development team, a dedicated coffee call center, and a new logistics platform exclusively for the coffee business. Although the changes increased the cost of implementing the business, they overcame the mismatch of resources and incentives and, in turn, generated much higher sales and profitability.

Because of the perceived expedience of the build mode, executives often choose it even when it makes little sense. If your internal resources fall far short of the target or your competitors are much stronger than you in the focal resource, you are almost always well advised to search outside—or, at the very least, supplement internal with external resources. In one of our surveys, 65 percent of the executives reported that insurmountable, severe challenges often arose when they attempted to develop new resources in-house. In turn, half the executives attributed failures to their inability to manage internal development—typically because they discovered too late that their firms lacked relevant technologies and personnel for internal projects.

What's more, when they do start to consider looking externally, firms often reflexively adopt the build mode as their primary or only option. The resulting losses—of time, money, momentum, and morale—are potentially costly. North American automakers GM and Ford historically fell into this trap. They were determined to develop and manufacture most components in their own subsidiaries, even though in-house knowledge of some technologies lagged behind the market and superior third-party options were available. This overreliance on internal development was one reason the firms lost their strong leads in the global auto industry. Certainly, they would often have been better served had they turned earlier to external sourcing.

Over time, firms that rely excessively on internal development fall prey to rigidity and inertia. Atari lost ground to Sony and Sega in the gaming industry during the mid-1990s, for instance, when it used internal development in attempting to keep the Atari Jaguar at the front of the market in software, core hardware, and accessories such as game controllers. Netscape, meanwhile, lost ground to Microsoft's Internet Explorer by focusing on internal skills to develop the inferior Navigator 4 browser rather than searching externally for new skills that would help it respond to Microsoft's advances. Similarly, Compaq lost its substantial position in PCs during the 1980s: though it attempted to develop various proprietary drivers and components, these could not compete with more flexible systems from competitors that combined best-of-market components in their laptops.

With so many examples of failure through the internal development route, why do companies persist so often and so long? Executives have several blind spots in assessing their firms' ability to develop new resources in-house.

Blind Spots: Why Do Firms Reflexively Choose Internal Development?

Executives making strategic resource decisions often choose internal development reflexively, without first assessing the resources they need to develop. They forget that no pathway is inherently superior to others; superiority is solely a function of context. And by failing to consider the context, executives default to history and habits, displaying a natural bias toward familiar paths. At companies that have internalized a long-standing preference for organic growth, therefore, executives are reluctant to seek needed resources externally and so fall into the implementation trap, believing that success is a matter of devoting enough money and hard work on internal projects. For these executives, the dynamic is typically triggered in four ways: hubris about internal strengths, functional incentive structures based on growing budgets and power, a limited awareness of new external developments, and a lack of external sourcing skills.

Hubris

Executives tend to hold unreasonably high opinions of their firms' in-house skills versus those of competitors. There can, of course, be powerful reasons to rely on internal resources: people who have a stake in the company and deeply understand its business may hold a natural advantage over outsiders when it comes to obtaining new resources. The problem arises when a firm believes its advantage applies in all or most circumstances.

One of our student groups conducted a research project at an ignition-coil manufacturer in Indiana. The students—who had experience at a high-quality European plant—hoped to help the Indiana facility overcome quality problems identified through internal audits. The team documented that severe issues with ignition-coil development and production led to significant quality problems in cars with these coils installed. Managers and workers at the plant were asked to rate themselves, on a five-point scale (where 5 was "global leader"), on their quality and effectiveness. The average response was about 4.8. The employees had apparently overindulged in self-esteem—they had no idea how far behind they were.

Misalignment of Stakeholders' Incentives

We frequently encounter a mind-set that views internal development as competing with external sourcing. Across functions such as R&D, information technology (IT), and marketing, leaders believe that their job is to "keep on keeping on"—keep researchers researching, developers developing, and marketers marketing—whether or not it's the best use of company resources. This mind-set leads functional leaders to skew toward increasing the use of internal resources. Their unstated agenda may be to grow functional resources and head-count—and thereby increase their own power—rather than make sure the company stays at the forefront of competitive change. Such leaders therefore disregard external resources because doing so could, in effect, reduce the perceived value of the people they lead, the resources they create, and the power they hold. Such entrench-ment exacts a high price and will be discussed further later in the chapter.

The drug company Schering-Plough eventually lost its indepen-dence when internal development failed to duplicate the success of its blockbuster drug, Claritin—largely because in-house labs resisted efforts to consider outside alternatives. When it became apparent that the internally developed successor drug would not fill Claritin's space in the market, Schering-Plough brought in new leadership. In a bid to recover, it allied with competitor Merck to codevelop an anti-cholesterol drug, which generated only moderate sales. With no blockbusters on the market or in the pipeline, Schering-Plough could not continue as an independent company; Merck acquired it in 2009.

Interestingly, Merck likewise had a history of strong bias toward internal development. In the early 2000s, it too found itself with a very short pipeline of viable new drug candidates. The company was able to restock its pipeline only after senior management squelched in-house labs' resistance to external sourcing as a com-plement to internal development. Merck expanded its sourcing strategy to include more active licensing, alliances, and small-scale acquisitions (see chapter 3). Unlike Schering-Plough—which waited too long to save itself—Merck learned to search outside its own boundaries.

Limited Horizons

Without meaning to, businesses sometimes become too inwardly focused. The world shrinks around them. Leaders grow accustomed to using traditional internal resources that reflect a limited set of suppliers, competitors, and market opportunities. Executives may not recognize that growing technical and market strength beyond their traditional purview might hold new opportunities for external sourcing.

For example, during the 1960s and 1970s, North American and European auto manufacturers missed the emergence of lean production in Japan. Present-day examples of growing resources include environmental technologies in China and financial services in Africa. Many businesses in the developed world myopically limit themselves globally by neglecting emerging markets as sources of new external opportunities.

Misaligned incentives and limited horizons often go together, as our case study of an established telecom business illustrates. The firm was struggling to develop a new data communication business. One of the senior executives highlighted conflicts between the new data business and engineers from the dominant voice business: "For a long time, most research funds were devoted to circuit technology, the dominant activity. But Internet development challenges this logic. The major issue is the intellectual blinders that most engineers wear as we move to intelligent networks; it is hard for our engineers to think beyond their circuit technology background to be able to adjust to this emerging business."

Many established companies face similar issues in obtaining adequate resources for growing business areas. IBM routinely missed new technologies and market opportunities during the 1980s and 1990s. An internal report documenting how the company failed to capture value from twenty-nine emerging technologies and businesses identified several reasons for the failure: too much emphasis on execution efficiency and short-term results, a related focus on current markets and existing offerings, and a tendency to assess growth opportunities using the same process and performance metrics applied to mature businesses.

These factors worked well enough in mature markets, but they limited IBM's ability to explore and develop new businesses. The challenge was compounded by the company's dominant ethos in the 1980s and 1990s: the idea, as one executive expressed it to us, that "We do it best." For many years, IBM placed most of its development bets internally. This is one reason for the company's slide back into the pack of computer firms, which left it struggling badly in the early 1990s. Only when it expanded its sourcing options—while learning to create and manage business experimentation—did IBM regain its stride. It continued to develop products internally—and indeed revitalized its ability to launch new products and businesses—but also actively sought in-licenses, alliances, and acquisitions for key parts of its evolving resource base.

Lack of External Sourcing Skills

Finally, many firms simply do not develop the skills needed to identify opportunities for external sourcing. Firms that have traditionally focused on organic growth are seldom adept at seeking and exploiting external resources.

In one of our studies, for instance, 48 percent of the executives reported that they used internal development rather than external modes, simply because they lacked the skills required to learn from external partners. Only 30 percent of the surveyed firms had systematically tried to screen and evaluate third-party resources from contracts, alliances, or acquisitions. One telecom executive noted that his firm's lack of a developed discipline for seeking and obtaining external resources had contributed to its overreliance on internal development.

Are Your Internal Resources Relevant?

The main weapon against internal-development blind spots is an honest assessment of how relevant your internal resources are at bridging the resource gap. Companies that choose to build new resources presume that their in-house capacity can fill resource gaps in a timely and cost-effective manner. Assessing resource relevance is challenging because companies often focus on a narrow set of criteria—for example, those that emphasize technological know-how. But relevance actually covers a broad spectrum of a firm's resources: technical knowledge, go-to-market capabilities, and organizational systems and values.

This multidimensional notion of resource relevance generates many shades of gray. As several corporate development heads told us, seldom does a clear-cut trigger lead them to choose external sourcing over internal development. Nonetheless, executives must ultimately make concrete decisions amid the shades of gray, evaluating the advantages and disadvantages of their firm's knowledge base and organization in light of the targeted resources.

To assess how relevant your internal resources are, focus on two dimensions (figure 2-1). *Knowledge fit* is how closely your existing knowledge base aligns with the targeted resources—that is, the exploitable compatibility between new and existing resources— together with the strength of your existing resources. *Organizational fit* is the compatibility of your established systems and values with those needed to develop the targeted resources. Many executives recognize the importance of knowledge fit, but too few carefully consider organizational fit. Most of the established telecom firms we studied had the

FIGURE 2–1

Internal development versus external sourcing

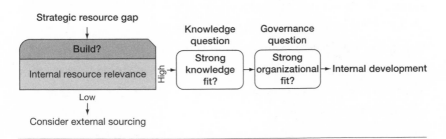

technical skills to develop new data communication businesses, but did not recognize how their organizational context—structures, incentives, cultural values, and control systems—would interfere with developing the new resources.

Knowledge Question: Do the Targeted Resources Fit Your Current Knowledge Base?

You need to determine whether your company's functional capabilities— such as R&D, marketing skills, and production processes—provide a relevant base upon which to create targeted resources quickly and effectively. Knowledge fit involves both closeness to the targeted resources and strength relative to other firms.

Resource closeness

The first step is to assess the closeness between your established knowledge base and the target resources. When closeness is high, a firm can usually develop the resources internally. Conversely, when the resources do not closely match your existing knowledge base, you should look outside. Without sufficient closeness and supporting internal competencies, internal development is very challenging.

Pursuing organic growth often means training existing people as well as hiring and integrating others with relevant backgrounds. Training is a challenge when targeted resources differ from existing ones. Personnel must absorb new knowledge, adjust their skills, and seek unfamiliar information by forming new networks. One executive we interviewed stressed these difficulties—even for highly motivated individuals: "Even when a manager from the traditional 'voice' environment of the telecom industry is willing to dedicate resources and time to developing new data communication skills, his mind-set is still somewhere else. He became a manager because he succeeded in his prior voice environment. His personal contacts are also in that environment."

The implication is that such a manager would have difficulty rising to the same level of performance in the data business as someone brought in from outside: "These people would not be as efficient at running a data business as somebody who has always been in the data world, created a start-up, knows the market and the players."

Similarly, it is challenging to evaluate and then train outside talent who could support an internal initiative. One executive told us, "We discovered that the marketing people we hired from a consumer-goods company did not understand the complexities of the telecom business. They're not selling their usual consumer products, and we didn't know enough about marketing to teach them how to market in the telecom context."

The head of digital transformation at a leading print media company told us that the firm preferred organic growth when the targeted product was close to the firm's core products and when the firm had commensurate expertise and scale in the targeted business. But with online products, the company found the difference between digital and legacy resources so great that the gap could only be bridged with immediate partnerships and acquisitions. Once it had secured external resources, the company supplemented them with internal efforts to upgrade digital skills through a combination of cross-training and new hires.

Resource strength

It is also crucial to weigh your strength in the targeted resource domain. Can you match or surpass other firms? Can you develop the needed resources faster, more cheaply, and at a higher quality than can other firms—whether competitors or potential resource suppliers? Even if the resources you need relate closely to your existing knowledge base, you cannot develop competitively viable resources if your company lags behind competitors and emerging innovators.

A senior executive at a global consumer-goods company cautioned that even high internal skills sometimes prove to be insufficient: "The question to ask is how far can you stretch and adapt your resources, versus recognizing that the time, effort, energy, and investment to convert them and build new capabilities might be higher than simply acquiring them . . . Related capabilities and resources in an adjacent product area might not be enough when you are entering a new market segment."

If your internal resource base is incomplete or out of date, it might be weaker than that of your peers. A lack of ongoing investments, the gradual erosion of knowledge, or a sudden shift in the targeted resource domain can all cause insufficiencies. If so, you will need to pursue more radical external sourcing options. Besides catching up with state-of-the-art knowledge, you must also bolster supporting systems and capabilities—for example, the marketing skills needed to increase customer awareness and build your brand's visibility in the targeted domain.

The head of corporate development at a leading European telecom firm—which acquired three US data networking companies to accelerate the development of the data business—noted significant transition challenges: "We were slow to understand the data environment. We had to make acquisitions not only to get good technologies, but also [to obtain] the whole set of data skills. We needed to ally with people who know the market, have always been in the data environment, have network knowledge, and know the type of people to look for."

Again, it is easy to overestimate the strength of your internal resources. You must thoughtfully benchmark yourself against relevant competitors and even consider firms beyond traditional industry boundaries. As possible outlier candidates, you might consider firms that have created important advances likely to disrupt your industry. For instance, cloud-computing vendors are now spawning technical advances and business-model innovations that are highly relevant for firms in the traditional hardware and software sectors of the computing industry.

Governance Question: Do the Targeted Resources Fit Your Current Organization?

Firms often struggle even when launching internal projects for which they possessed relevant technical and commercial skills. The projects generated substantial conflicts within their existing organizations and were ultimately destined to fail. New internal resources must fit well with the organizational processes of your firm. Otherwise, they will be resisted by almost everyone who has a stake in the old practices, culture, and processes. The strongest resistance arises when the targeted resources threaten your current resources with obsolescence.

Fit with your current systems

A majority of the executives we interviewed reckoned that internal development was most appropriate when the needed capabilities would bring only minor changes to the organization. Conversely, a firm whose organizational models align poorly with targeted resources should consider obtaining external systems rather than struggling to adapt what it has; the firm will then more easily integrate external resources and associated systems—particularly when market pressures provide a sense of urgency, motivating buy-in from employees and other stakeholders.

For example, the Indian IT consulting firm Infosys licensed new software technology when it began to offer health sector services. Even though the new services called for technical skills similar to those used in its existing business, Infosys chose an external source because health-care consulting required a substantially different organizational structure. By entering into a licensing agreement, Infosys achieved an immediate presence in the new market segment. Moreover, the company avoided organizational conflicts that would surely have arisen had it instead tried to adapt its current offerings.

Firms may also benefit from sourcing externally when they enter a new market segment—one that has different organizational requirements—and do not want to confuse their sales channels and brands. For instance, when Carrier, a unit of United Technologies Group, decided to develop an environmentally friendly refrigeration system for its core premium market in Europe, it did so internally. But it looked outside to obtain more conventional technology to use in a lower-end refrigeration system for the rest of the market. In 2009, Carrier bought Swedish manufacturer Green & Cool, which had appropriate technology and was already serving this market. Clearly, Carrier could have used its internal skills to build a full range of products, but it instead sought to avoid organizational conflicts about potential cannibalization and channel conflict, while preserving its core premium brand as it experimented with new market segments.

Nonetheless, do not *always* duck conflict. Sometimes it is best to tackle it head-on. Indeed, internal conflict can generate useful insights that help you build stronger resources and avoid being trapped in outmoded models. As long as you can control the dissonance, internal debate can produce benefits that external sources won't. Still, you should pick such opportunities carefully; even the most productive conflicts will require substantial time and effort to manage.

Internal competition

Some executives—especially at firms heavily invested in existing, long-established technologies and business models—misguidedly decline to develop new resources. The reason? They want to avoid internal competition, to preserve the value of existing resources, and thus retain their power. In the telecom industry, voice-networking groups have been loath to relinquish power to their data-networking counterparts. One of our telecom respondents reported that in some firms, "investments and resource allocations in data technologies have been postponed or limited due to this internal competition."

Likewise, media companies frequently faced internal resistance when attempting to parlay existing print-media skills into the digital domain. A media executive from a company that combined its print and online newsrooms told us that journalists from the print newspapers removed their names from online articles—which they regarded as lower in quality, credibility, and sophistication and as a threat to their traditional skills. The cultural and competitive divide between the print and digital units hampered the diffusion of skills across the whole organization.

Such opposition is most heated when targeted capabilities compete with or replace the firm's existing capabilities. In theory, targeted capabilities might appear close to an organization's existing capabilities. In practice, however, entrenched individuals may resist developing and using new capabilities to retain their power. This happens most often when the new capabilities gain prominence and value seemingly at the expense of old ones. No matter the industry, vested interests will be slow to free up resources and allocate them to new activities. Cross-functional coordination will be hampered by competition for time, attention, resources, and control.

Before your business can develop new resources—especially those that threaten some stakeholders' livelihoods—it will need to overcome these most challenging and potentially damaging internal barriers. Your company may have to change the culture, values, or working habits of the incumbent organization on the ground floor and integrate the new work styles of recently hired employees.

An executive who had recently jumped from a computer company to an old-guard firm in another industry told us that his new company did poorly at both attracting and integrating outsiders. He saw this as a major obstacle to upgrading the firm's skills: "I was brought on board to build up the marketing organization. Given what they wanted me to do, I was a perfect fit for the company. But I don't think I've ever really broken through. It is a major hurdle! . . . I always felt like an outsider. When I tried to do anything, I always had to fight—even though I had the full support of the senior managers."

Entrenched internal teams commonly avoid competition, to protect themselves. Change will never succeed across an organization if it can't be made to work in the lower echelons. Clearly, you will benefit if you can push your existing culture to adopt competitive internal projects. But if this is not possible, you will waste time, money, and competitive opportunity by trying to do so. As we discuss below, searching for external resources is often a way to short-circuit internal opposition.

Implementation challenges

Your company may be lucky enough to have extra resources available to tackle new projects with ease. More likely, though, you will first need to free up currently assigned human and financial resources before pursuing new internal projects. New projects typically disrupt existing activities. If the company unit and personnel best suited for your project are already heavily burdened, you must find a way forward that does not compromise important work already under way.

Consider whether you can shut down lower-priority projects to accommodate the new task. In most companies, many once-important tasks continue well past their expiration dates. Some business areas are obsolete; others that once gained competitive advantages from internal expertise, but have since lost some of their strategic luster, might now be moved to outside service providers. Do not be constrained by past priorities. A careful triage will likely identify talent that could be freed up to work more productively on your new project. For example, many pharmaceutical firms sold off older production and development activities to focus current internal development on emerging high-value areas of biological and therapeutic products.

Also pay attention to the challenge of identifying and interconnecting the right internal people, and then managing their various contributions. Never assume that participants in projects involving multiple units will collaborate seamlessly. Their activities will need active management and coordination. For example, incentives may need to be adjusted to drive effective collaboration. Among our telecom industry respondents, only 40 percent reported that their company promoted active internal networking by adopting incentives to share best practices and capabilities with other units. Job rotation across units and an active internal labor market existed in only about one-third of the firms, and only one-third were aware that internal resources could be made readily available to other staff or units.

Firms have used several approaches to address these challenges. Johnson & Johnson sought a more efficient flow of resources and innovations by creating an internal ventures group. Its role was to facilitate collaborative R&D and commercialization projects among its more than two hundred subsidiaries. And in the digital transformation of a leading publisher we studied, its corporate center assumed the role of promoting enterprise-wide innovation with an emphasis on connecting resources across business units.

Implications for Your Resource Sourcing Strategy

If your best efforts fail to assemble an unencumbered in-house project team, you must then begin considering external sourcing options. Figure 2-2 summarizes the conclusions that arise along the resource pathway. The answers to the knowledge and governance questions will help you determine whether to develop targeted resources internally or externally. Internal development is most appropriate when targeted resources align with both your existing resources and your organization.

FIGURE 2–2

Internal resource relevance and resource sourcing options

Governance question: organizational fit of the targeted resources?

		High	Low
Knowledge question: knowledge fit of the targeted resources?	High	Internal resource relevance: high *Close-knit projects* Internal development	Internal resource relevance: partial *Homeless projects* Consider external sourcing *Alternative*: consider internal exploratory environment
	Low	Internal resource relevance: partial *Resourceless projects* Consider external sourcing *Alternative*: consider internal exploratory environment	Internal resource relevance: low *Unrelated projects* Consider external sourcing

We call these *close-knit* projects. In other combinations of internal resource and organizational fit, you will typically benefit by conducting an initial search for outside resources. If external sources are available, they usually provide a more effective means of obtaining the targeted resources. Chosen well and managed properly, outside resources present your firm with a learning opportunity to overcome its knowledge gaps and organizational limits.

The upper left and lower right cells in figure 2-2 are straightforward cases, whereas the other two cells are more complex but nonetheless offer opportunities to build your internal capabilities. Let's look at all four cases.

Close-knit projects

The resource relevance of close-knit projects is high on both axes (existing knowledge base and organizational fit). For example, Eli Lilly developed the drug Zyprexa within its existing research labs, building on the skills it had used to develop Prozac. Resource fit was high because the new drug used existing technical expertise in central nervous system therapies, both in development and in clinical trials. Organizational fit was high because the new drug had a market similar to that of prior products, used compatible regulatory and marketing procedures, and used familiar evaluation techniques.

Unrelated projects

These projects are straightforward triggers for external sourcing. They arise when your relevant knowledge base is weak and the project would generate internal discord. Unrelated projects might always require external sourcing. But if the targeted resources are strategically important, you can leverage external experience to augment your resource base and organizational fit over time.

In practice, many unrelated projects become learning opportunities. For instance, Abbott Laboratories recently decided to expand its pharmaceutical business in India. The company chose not to develop the necessary marketing and regulatory systems internally. Despite Abbott's global strength in these areas—built through experience in North America, Europe, and elsewhere—it lacked knowledge of how to develop and market drugs in the Indian context. Organizational fit was low because the market required very different marketing, regulatory systems, and incentives from those in developed markets or even emerging markets such as China. As a result, Abbott acquired an Indian "branded generics" business. Beyond achieving immediate market penetration, Abbott expected that the acquisition would help it learn about the branded generic drugs business, thereby enhancing the company's global knowledge base and organizational capabilities.

Homeless projects

Projects like these have strong relevant internal knowledge, but the targeted resources fit poorly with organizational context. In such cases, it often makes sense to first search externally for straightforward alternatives.

If easy external solutions are unavailable, reconsider a variant of internal development: the creation of an internal exploratory environment, which can be an effective way of sidestepping organizational barriers to internal development. With this approach, corporations experiment with new resources in an internal organizational context that keeps the experiments protected from the firm's dominant cultural and other pressures. In the late 1990s, the Swedish company Telia created the Telia Light venture to develop its IP telephony at the periphery of its mainstream organization. (More examples of internal exploratory environments are presented in the next section.)

Even when an external source will satisfy your immediate resource needs, you might consider running this approach in tandem. External relationships can help you reduce organizational barriers to newly developed internal resources when an appropriate opportunity knocks. For instance, most telecom incumbents that wanted to develop VOIP (voice over Internet protocol) businesses turned to external sources. The companies were unwilling to develop internal capabilities that would surely challenge vested interests and sow conflict in the knowledge base, culture, and organization. Searching externally can thus be a way to borrow or buy targeted capabilities while also growing a critical mass of people with different skills. Over time, these skills and expertise infuse cultural change across the organization.

Resourceless projects

These projects have a weak knowledge base, but high organizational fit for operational routines and cultural values. For resourceless projects, an initial external search makes sense. Besides satisfying your immediate resource needs, external sourcing through borrowing or buying lets you learn and quickly integrate new functional skills. Your possession of a compatible organization will facilitate importing knowledge into the organization so that future development in that area can be internal.

When the semiconductor firm AMD wanted to integrate graphics processors with its core computer processors, it first considered an internal development project. The project was fully compatible with AMD's organizational context and values. But the necessary technical and market skills differed substantially from AMD's existing knowledge base. So AMD searched externally and purchased ATI Technologies, a Canadian graphics-processor company and a dominant player in that industry segment. AMD folded ATI into its AMD Graphics Products Group. Once AMD built internal competencies as a result of the acquisition, the firm removed the ATI brand from its graphics-processor products.

Beyond traditional means of enhancing internal competencies, some companies have recently learned to tap insight from their current and prospective customers. LEGO, the Danish toy producer, engages in a form of open innovation by encouraging "lead users" to become cocreators in product design. InnoCentive is an example of open innovation with an even broader set of external stakeholders.

Since 2006 (and in earlier years as part of Eli Lilly), InnoCentive has enlisted clients such as P&G and NASE to sponsor crowd-sourcing challenges for its roster of more than two hundred thousand "solvers." InnoCentive pays solvers cash awards for solutions that best meet clients' criteria. When there is no obvious traditional outside match, perhaps your resource needs can be met successfully by the crowd.

Internal Exploratory Environments

Important Routes to Novel Internal Changes

As discussed, when your firm lacks the relevant skills or organization to develop a targeted resource, an internal exploratory environment can generate information that may help resolve the uncertainties of a promising project and even lead to a breakthrough. In such an environment, people can experiment with projects radically different from their ongoing activities, or an independent unit is created to develop new resources outside the mainstream organization. Internal exploratory environments encompass both small-scale Skunk Works projects and larger-scale semi-autonomous units. These exploratory environments are often appropriate when there is no viable external source for a strategically important resource.

The general manager of an online business within a European company told us, "When we cannot acquire new resources on labor markets or from other firms, we experiment internally. We experiment, fail, and learn. We develop the strategy ourselves, by refining our practices within a *very loose framework*."

Internal exploratory environments are especially useful for homeless projects, where organizational tensions impede your use of relevant internal knowledge to create the targeted resources. Let's look at the two main variants of this approach.

Skunk Works projects are small-scale undertakings within an active operating unit. Such projects typically consist of one or a few people who work together on experiments to create new goods, services, processes, business models, or other innovations. Skunk Works projects are done in addition to the members' full-time jobs. Some projects are informal nights-and-weekends efforts that fly under the corporate radar and often divert resources from other projects, while others are active parts of a company's formal technology strategy.

Skunk Works projects have met with various levels of failure and success. During the early 1960s, Frito-Lay executive Arch West reportedly diverted money from other budgets for quiet research on a new product line, which eventually became Doritos, after higher-ups failed to share his enthusiasm for this variant of corn chips. Recognizing the creative potential of Skunk Works, businesses in growing numbers actively encourage employees to spend a portion of their time on self-driven experimentation. Whether sanctioned or off the radar, Skunk Works allow for small-scale explorations in which failures can be shut down easily and projects that show potential earn their way to increasing investments.

Engineers at GE's Yokagawa Medical Systems joint venture in Japan created a mobile magnetic resonance imaging (MRI) system in the 1980s by diverting budget and time from other projects—completely counter to their instructions from US leadership. Yet rather than fire the engineers when they unveiled their product, the company embraced the design as an important innovation. The mobile system became a major addition to GE's product line, essentially pushing its mobile imaging competitor, Diasonics, out of the MRI market.

There are many examples of successful Skunk Works as formal parts of technology strategy:

- 3M has long encouraged its people to explore innovations as part of their ongoing work; this practice helps the company continually refresh its product line.

- Google asks that staff members spend 20 percent of their time investigating independent ideas; the company estimates that as many as half its new products (including Gmail, Google News,

Orkut, and AdSense services) come from this Skunk Works time.

• Shell's "Game Changer" innovation model encourages employees to take time out of their regular schedules to work on projects that might lead to disruptive changes in the existing Shell business. Projects have ranged from new extraction technologies to new ocean drilling techniques to hydrogen fuel cell distribution models that would radically change the petroleum-based business model. When projects succeed, the company integrates them back into the core business. If a project is sufficiently successful and generates a sufficiently large market, Shell has the option of creating an entirely new division for the venture.

Semi-autonomous units are larger-scale ventures in which a company creates a separate operating unit that is typically empowered to draw resources from established units. Unlike Skunk Works, which may be formal or informal, semi-autonomous units almost always require a formal charter. But they resemble Skunk Works in that they allow for experimentation away from the core. This degree of freedom limits the risk that a firm's existing activities and pressures could constrain innovation efforts that rely on highly unconventional methods. When semi-autonomous units fail, as they often do, they are easy to shut down or sell. When they succeed, their successes can be integrated into the company. Some successes are so significant, they change the direction of a company.

Semi-autonomous units can be safe havens for new ventures, sheltering them from an assortment of threats. We observed their use by incumbent firms that faced internal social conflict when developing new resources. For example, one European company decided to set up its data business in the United States, where it was easier both to attract the type of people it sought and to offer a more attractive corporate environment—including more generous compensation packages than those in its home market. Striking such bargains at home—where, for example, only top managers were offered stock options—would have created substantial conflict with employees and unions. To insulate the new unit even more from the rest of the company, the US subsidiary did not use the name of the parent firm.

When Hewlett-Packard decided, in the 1970s, to experiment with PC laser and inkjet printers, it considered buying several companies with a printer technology base. After assessing the targets carefully, HP decided they were overpriced relative to the strength of their technologies. But the company did not want to build a new printer business internally. The business model for printers would have conflicted strongly with the incumbent businesses: new design timelines and criteria would clash with customary ways of evaluating and providing resources for new projects, and printer sales channels would differ substantially from those serving HP's minicomputers.

Quite simply, the PC printer business could have been squashed by the established divisions before getting off the ground. So HP set up a semi-autonomous unit, based in Idaho and Washington State, well away from the corporate core in California.

HP didn't leave the new business entirely on its own. It assigned leadership of the initiative to a highly influential senior executive who reported directly to the board and was empowered to obtain whatever resources the unit needed to grow. The company possessed some of the relevant skills in electronics and assembly for designing new printers, but it lacked other key resources (most notably, toner technology). So the fledgling printer unit developed a focused partnership with Canon, the global leader in toner technology. Once the printer business was a demonstrated success, HP gradually recentered its business around printers, eventually selling off its once-core scientific instruments business.

Similarly, IBM set up a semi-autonomous business unit—in Florida, far from its New York headquarters—to launch its new PC business. The company's resource strength was high, with strong relevant skills in electronics and assembly. These skills would allow it to create a new type of computer more effectively than competitors could. But the organizational fit was low. IBM sold "heavy iron" main-frame computers predominantly to business enterprises. The PC would begin as a consumer product requiring a substantially different business model. (Businesses didn't purchase PCs in volume until the mid- to late 1980s.) Compared with IBM's expensive mainframes, the PC was a small-ticket item that would call for new sales channels. But once the PC business demonstrated enough success to quell internal resistance, IBM absorbed it back into the core company.

A further example is not a new business per se, but a formal mechanism for developing and acquiring new businesses. PepsiCo recently created a semi-autonomous unit dubbed PepsiCo New Ventures. Its mandate is to pursue opportunities in high-growth areas beyond the company's traditional core—for example, more health-conscious products such as juices, cereal bars, and low-fat dairy offerings. PepsiCo wanted to use the dedicated unit to create novel lines of business. Earlier attempts to develop such products within the mainstream organization had failed, both because resources were lacking and because of insufficient management bandwidth to devote to emerging products. Besides incubation skills, PepsiCo New Ventures will also help screen potential targets and conduct acquisitions in promising new market segments. Once any of its projects hits a certain size, it either becomes a stand-alone business or is integrated into an existing unit.

Like any other high-risk or speculative initiative, semi-autonomous units can fail, sometimes exacting a high cost. General Motors created the Saturn division during the 1980s as a means of experimenting with new ways to assemble and sell cars. The division initially succeeded in both design quality and market acceptance. But strong internal and external pressure from traditional stakeholders (company leadership, representatives, dealerships, and suppliers) hampered GM's efforts to integrate Saturn's successful innovations back into the core company. The same organizational pressures that had led GM to launch Saturn as a semi-autonomous unit ultimately impeded GM's ability to integrate the successes from the experiment.

A Powerful but Underused Strategy

At their best, internal exploratory environments allow you to leverage your existing knowledge, create new resources, and control what you create. You can often complement the exploratory work of these environments with contracts, alliances, and acquisitions. Used selectively and effectively, internal exploratory environments will help overcome knowledge shortfalls while building up the internal support for the new resources.

Despite the failure of some internal exploratory environment efforts and the difficulties of integrating successful semi-autonomous units—often considered "bastard" siblings within the organization—it is nonetheless puzzling that so many firms neglect their potential. They can be a highly effective means of nurturing innovations that would otherwise be squashed by traditional organizational pressures. In our telecom study, only about one-third of respondents used some form of internal exploratory environment. Perhaps that seems like a lot. But the 1990s and 2000s were rampant with disruptive technology changes that provoked loud internal conflicts, as old and new models clashed. If ever there was a time to innovate successfully—and to protect innovations from the winds of internal opposition—this was it!

In practice, many businesses underutilize the internal exploratory environment option because their leaders suppose that Skunk Works and semi-autonomous units will be too difficult to manage or because leaders fear losing strategic control to lower-level operating staff within their company. Clearly, companies must manage these environments thoughtfully, setting limits on the time and budget that can be diverted from core activities. Yet the possible payoffs from a game-changing innovation should be irresistible. A success on the order of HP's printer business—which transformed the company for decades—would almost certainly have been impossible without the internal exploratory environment model. Even smaller-scale successes can successfully expand product lines and services. Internal exploratory environments present a tantalizing opportunity to pursue a hybrid form of internal development for both homeless and resourceless projects that nonetheless hold high strategic promise.

Assessment Tool and Summary

The questions in table 2-1 reflect the key ideas of this chapter and will help you assess whether your present knowledge base and organization are relevant to filling your resource gap. Your answers should alert you if your choice of a pathway is inconsistent with the nature of these present resources.

If most of your responses are yes (i.e., the targeted resources fit both your existing knowledge base and your organization), you should consider internal development. However, if most of your responses are no, you should consider external sourcing options before embarking on what will likely be a very challenging internal development process.

Of course, choosing between internal and external sourcing approaches is not a onetime decision. Smart companies periodically revisit the question as they grow a new business. When General Electric entered the CT scanner business, the company licensed technology from an early entrant to complement its own technology. GE considered its existing radiography skills insufficient for thriving in the new market. After the company expanded its knowledge base, it continued with internal development of highly successful CT instruments.

Many executives believe they can make any internal project work if only they achieve a stellar implementation. Consequently, they push employees to work harder and longer. We are often asked to recommend state-of-the-art techniques to help leaders manage complicated internal projects whose required resources far exceed their knowledge base or involve substantial organizational disruption. Of course, there are many effective techniques for coordinating, managing, and eventually integrating internal projects. But those techniques can't help an ill-chosen path succeed. Many such projects are unsuitable for the build mode. The fundamental issue is not implementation; it is selection

TABLE 2-1

Internal resource relevance

Knowledge question: knowledge fit of targeted resources		No	Yes
Resource closeness	Are our established knowledge base and skills similar to the targeted resources?		
	Do we have or can we have access to complementary resources that we will need to support the targeted resources?		
	Can we train or hire the people we need to develop the targeted resources?		
Resource strength	Can we develop the targeted resources more cheaply or with higher quality than other firms?		
	Can we develop the targeted resources faster than other firms?		
Governance question: organizational fit of targeted resources			
Fit with current systems	Do the targeted resources fit our current systems of incentives and culture?		
	Is there low risk of creating a cultural divide between the targeted resources and our legacy resources?		
Internal competition	Can the targeted resources coexist with our legacy resources without significant conflict?		
Implementation challenges	Do we have extra resources, or can we free up resources to develop the targeted resources internally?		
	Can we connect and coordinate our internal resources to help execute the new resource-development project?		

Answer each question about the knowledge fit and organizational fit of the targeted resources. If most of your responses are yes, consider internal development (*build* mode). If most of your responses are no, consider external sourcing options.

capability—choosing a sourcing mode that suits the project well enough that implementation techniques have a reasonable chance of succeeding.

Internal development is most appropriate when you have a relevant internal knowledge base *and* organizational fit. These factors combine to create a close-knit project—provided internal efforts have both the necessary personnel and the financial resources. If you are missing either the internal knowledge base or a good fit between the targeted resources and your organization, then you should search outside.

Indeed, external search almost always makes sense if your project would make internal development challenging. Even so, there may not always be viable external solutions. (This is more likely to happen when the resources you target are in an emergent knowledge domain or business model.) In such cases, you might reconsider internal development—especially if the target opportunity has high potential value for your organization. You should weigh the benefits of creating an internal exploratory environment as a way of sidestepping knowledge or organizational barriers.

In this chapter, we have focused on the first steps along the resource pathways framework, asking questions that will help you decide whether to develop targeted resources internally or search for them externally. Chapter 3 describes the framework's next steps and will help you decide between the external options of basic contracts and more complicated alliance relationships.

When to Borrow via Contract

Basic Contract Versus Alliance

Once you've determined that you need to seek resources externally, you must consider what kind of outside sourcing mode to use: basic contract, alliance, or acquisition. Faced with these three options, many firms jump straight to an acquisition. When the target firm has the desired resources, they assume that ownership through acquisition is a prerequisite of competitive advantage. And yet borrowing resources via a basic contract or an alliance could prove to be an adequate—even a superior—pathway.

You neglect these lower-intensity borrowing options at your peril. Used appropriately, basic contracts and alliances provide access to third-party resources under more flexible terms and at lower risks and costs than an acquisition. As noted earlier, M&A is inevitably an expensive and complicated entanglement that should only be pursued as a last resort. Overemphasizing the need for control and leaping unnecessarily to acquire a company can waste time and investment capital. And you will miss opportunities to learn from a variety of independent partners and will ultimately diminish your ability to refresh core resources. In this chapter, we explore the trade-offs between basic contracts and more complicated ways of obtaining external resources.

The first and most straightforward external option is a basic contract, an arm's-length agreement that spells out the terms of exchange of discrete resources. Basic contracts provide specified rights to a resource through a sales agreement, or more limited rights via a licensing agreement. While other more complicated sourcing modes (alliances and acquisitions, discussed later in the book) are also governed by contracts, this chapter addresses contractual relationships with relatively straightforward conditions. For the sake of simplicity, we will often refer to basic contracts as *contracts* or *contracting*.

Through a good contracting strategy, you can shop freely for desirable resources from third parties without incurring the costs of acquiring and integrating an entire organization or the complexities of managing an ongoing alliance. Contracting strategy is most effective when coupled with strong internal capabilities to successfully absorb new knowledge into the firm.

Since the early 1990s, licenses and other basic contracts have become a key part of growth strategy in the life-sciences sector. As discussed, some pharmaceutical firms now commonly license the rights to register and market other companies' drugs in particular geographic markets. Drug companies also select desired compounds from external innovators to supplement their internal R&D pipelines. Novartis, GlaxoSmithKline (GSK), Merck, and Sanofi-Aventis, among others, have done this quite actively. (See the sidebar "Merck's Outside Strategy.") Externally sourced, midstage drug candidates can represent as much as 50 percent of the largest pharmaceutical companies' total pipelines. In the telecom industry, a consortium of firms (including Apple, Microsoft, and Research In Motion) made headlines in 2011 when it bought up six thousand patents held by the bankrupt Canadian vendor Nortel Networks. Deals like that can be bargains when compared with a far more complicated alliance—and certainly an outright acquisition.

MERCK'S OUTSIDE STRATEGY

Using External Sourcing to Revitalize the Drug Pipeline

The pharmaceutical company Merck increased its use of external sourcing for new-drug development during the 2000s in an effort to reinforce its internal product pipeline. Its success highlights the value of focused licensing.

Long respected for its exceptional internal drug-development capability, Merck had developed many breakthrough products in its own labs: the cardiac drugs Mevacor and Zocor, the HIV/AIDS drug Efavirenz, the osteoporosis drug Fosamax, and vaccines such as Gardasil. But in 2002, Merck reviewed its clinical pipeline and found substantial cause for concern. Only one new drug had been approved in the United States that year, with one other under review. In addition, there were seven drugs in Phase 3 clinical trials, five in Phase 2, and only four in Phase 1 (the earliest stage of clinical trials involving humans). Although the roster of drugs in clinical trials would have been a solid base for a smaller company, it could not support a multibillion-dollar global leader like Merck—especially since some of the drugs would undoubtedly fail their trials.

The review led the company to rethink its dominant emphasis on internal development. All but two of the candidates in the 2002 pipeline had emerged from Merck's in-house labs. Disinclined to trim its investments in internal development, Merck nevertheless decided to ratchet up its use of external sourcing to increase the number of candidates. By 2006, the pipeline was dramatically fuller, with twenty-eight candidates (five external) in Phase 1; eighteen (six external) in Phase 2; four (one external) in Phase 3; and five (one external) under review by the FDA. To be sure, Merck had also turned up the development heat internally. But overall, it had identified more than a dozen license and other external opportunities to complement its in-house development.

Merck's use of licenses had two defining characteristics: first, each license targeted products beyond the firm's existing technical base while also complementing existing product lines, such as specialty cancer, psychiatric disorder, and cardiovascular drugs. Second, the licenses with drug originators were all negotiated as focused codevelopment contracts. These relationships often reinforced internal projects, and some of these licenses later became acquisitions.

Merck's successful strategy was to use licensing not as a substitute for, but as a powerful complement to, internal development and other forms of sourcing. Merck continues to invest heavily in its internal labs, spending substantially more money on R&D in 2011 than it did in 2006. But few firms in any industry can count on responding to competitive challenges purely with internal projects. Instead, they need to develop the ability to both complement and enrich internal skills and capabilities by tapping outside sources.

The Nortel deal remains the exception, not the rule. Our approach to choosing an external sourcing mode is simple: *reserve the most integrative and costly external sourcing modes for cases where absolutely nothing else will work.* There is no reason to employ more complex modes if the conditions suit a simpler contract, such as a technology licensing agreement. As a telecom executive told us, "whenever possible, go for the cheapest way: the basic contract or the one-shot transaction."

The cost of a relationship with your resource partner rises with the strength of the linkage. Such costs extend well beyond pure financial expense. As your relationship with a partner deepens, you will often need to devote substantial time and attention to the relationship, which can drain management focus away from current activities. Moreover, an alliance can carry a greater risk of intellectual property loss (via resource leakage and copying) than would a basic contract.

Basic contracts and alliances are two distinct forms of borrowing resources. Examples of basic contracts include licensing technology or products from other firms, agreeing on royalties to use others' proprietary assets, and out-licensing to others the right to sell your products, sometimes with full rights to use the resources (essentially full-scale purchases) and at other times with relatively straightforward contingencies (such as limiting use to particular products or markets).

In its simplest form, a basic contract is a passive relationship. The contractor, having granted permission to the contractee to exploit its intellectual property, is not required to do anything else; it simply collects initial payments, royalties, and any other specified sums. The contractee has firm access only to technology that exists when the agreement is signed.

Strategic alliances, on the other hand, are a much more active form of borrowing; they usually involve licenses and other contracts, but also extend well beyond those agreements. With codevelopment alliances, for instance, the partners agree to further develop jointly the intellectual property that is the object of their alliance. The licensor is therefore entitled to a larger share of milestone payments and royalties than would otherwise be the case.

Resource-seeking firms need to recognize conditions that favor basic contracts. Contracts can be difficult; many executives liken them to blind dating. Firms may know little about available external resources, their true market value, or the prospects for obtaining comparable resources from alternate suppliers and thus should apply due diligence when using contracts to source new resources. Nevertheless, the issues are often manageable and the benefits plentiful.

Even in emerging markets—where firms from the developed world have historically avoided basic license agreements—intellectual property laws governing patents, copyrights, and marketing exclusivity agreements are increasingly being enforced, although with substantial remaining problems. This is especially true as more local companies develop proprietary technical and market expertise that benefits from such protections. As these changes have taken hold, resource contracts are being negotiated with growing confidence in many emerging markets.

In this chapter, we'll describe the criteria favoring or discouraging the use of contacts to acquire resources. But first, let's look at some of the cognitive and behavioral biases that discourage managers from using contracts more often.

Blind Spots: Why Do Firms Overlook Basic Contracts?

Why do many firms jump to form alliances or make acquisitions without even thinking of contracting? Our research and experience suggest several blind spots: executives are obsessed with control, misuse M&A as a strategic shortcut, exaggerate the frictions that could arise within contractual arrangements, and draw the wrong lessons from prior contract failures.

Obsessing About Control

A firm often goes straight to more complex sourcing modes because it overemphasizes the need to control its resource partners and exclude rivals. It believes that a license deal would force it to give up too much revenue and intellectual property. Many firms—especially those that historically emphasize internal development and hence regard control as a given—overestimate how much strategic control they really need. Consequently, they miss opportunities for profitable third-party relationships.

Firms tend to believe, often mistakenly, that sharing a revenue stream, such as through a license for a specific product, is more expensive than paying the many costs of M&A, including those related to valuing and integrating acquisitions. Firms that have learned to use the full array of external arrangements hold an advantage over those that neglect licensing and instinctively pursue acquisitions.

Bombardier has sometimes struggled to compete with Embraer in pricing its regional jets because the former company has historically been less willing than its Brazilian competitor to contract for even general components. Bombardier has sometimes underestimated the costs of either developing and producing components internally or acquiring suppliers. The overlooked costs of contract alternatives—such as the cost of retooling facilities and managing complicated internal projects and acquisition-integration programs—can far outweigh the anticipated benefits. As noted in chapter 2, many North American auto companies fell into similar traps of developing and producing components that they could have contracted to outside suppliers at substantially lower costs and higher quality.

Wanting a Shortcut

In their mania for control, executives often fall for M&A as a seductive shortcut. To be sure, a well-conceived and well-executed acquisition can slingshot a firm past its competitors by several years. Best of all, it gains control of the resource supplier.

But acquisitions often fail. In fast-changing environments, where agility is paramount, M&A can be a slow way to respond. Acquisitions can leave a firm muscle-bound, ultimately constraining its ability to satisfy its evolving resource needs and adaptively pursue its growth.

Some banks have sought to grow revenues by selling insurance products. Banks enjoy regular contacts with customers; each physical or online interaction provides a potential opportunity to cross-sell insurance-based products and services. Many banks have used M&A to quickly acquire the product capabilities and scale they need in the insurance market. However, few have succeeded. Indeed, Citigroup, ING, and others have lately been divesting their insurance arms.

These failures have awakened interest in contractual and joint-venture relationships, which recognize insurance as a complicated specialty. Through such arrangements, banks sell insurance products sourced from a third party or from a company that is often owned fifty-fifty by the bank and its chosen insurance partner. Typically, the insurer is responsible for managing risk, and the bank is responsible for distributing the product to customers. The partners may collaborate on branding and cross-selling activities, and both take a share of revenue and of profit or loss.

An alliance between Amazon.com and Toys "R" Us is another example of a company's falling for a seductive shortcut. The two companies joined forces in 2000 to codevelop an online toy-retailing business. Amazon.com viewed the relationship as an opportunity to learn the toy business and adapt it to an online setting. Toys "R" Us, on the other hand, viewed things more simply: it sought a new channel for its existing toy and children's products business and an expedient shortcut for beating rivals to the e-commerce trough.

In practice, Amazon.com gained much more from the alliance than did Toys "R" Us. The relationship provided a platform for expanding Amazon's online business, but had unwittingly created a competitor for Toys "R" Us. Indeed, the toy store sued Amazon in 2004, claiming that the online retailer had taken advantage of what it learned in the relationship to purchase its own lines of competing products and to allow other merchants to sell toys and baby products on the Amazon.com site. The suit was finally settled in 2009 with a payment of $51 million to Toys "R" Us—far less than the opportunity cost of having helped a competitor gain a strong market position.

In retrospect, Toys "R" Us was so eager to pursue its shortcut that it overlooked the threat to its own vital resources. The company would have been better off pursuing a more basic contract, not the deeper alliance that led to undesired knowledge leakage to Amazon.com. A simpler contract would have helped Toys "R" Us focus its activities on the sales channel while limiting knowledge transfer to Amazon.com about sourcing and product management. If Toys "R" Us ultimately found the relationship becoming more strategic, it could then have moved to an alliance in which it had a stronger position for engaging in the online business. Basic contractual agreements can help avoid knowledge loss and organizational trauma when relationships require only basic interactions.

Overestimating Frictions

Many executives, concerned about substantial frictions when they attempt to obtain discrete resources from third parties, are wary of venturing, uninformed and unprotected, into a contractual market.

(One outlier strategy for avoiding both frictions and costs—at least in the short term—is to look for *legally unprotected* resources that can be freely appropriated. See the sidebar "Free Resources.")

Of course, frictions are often real. Markets for resources may simply not exist or exist only in embryonic form. Contractual partners may act opportunistically in their own interests—especially if an agreement is too complicated to cover all contingencies effectively with a basic contract—and firms are consequently often reluctant to trust external parties. Indeed, a contractee may lack clear knowledge of what the contractor is selling or what value a licensed resource may have in another geographic or product market. The cost of searching for partners can be high if information is scarce or sellers are hard to find.

Once a firm has identified a viable partner, the partner won't necessarily want to sell or license its resources; instead it might seek to capture

FREE RESOURCES

The Costs and Benefits of Copying

A somewhat murky no-man's-land of resources consists of properties that are not patented, trademarked, or otherwise legally protected. Such resources are therefore available to be copied, modified, and used—whether with their creators' or owners' explicit permission or by default, owing to their unprotected state. If you find desirable resources that fall outside of legal safeguards, you may simply want to copy and build on them to suit your own needs and strategies.

Nevertheless, keep your imitation activities aboveboard. There are good reasons to be cautious. You—like your partners and competitors—will be tempted to take advantage of weak legal environments. But short-term advantages that firms gain through such opportunism can create longer-term disadvantages—for instance, when desirable would-be partners refuse to contract or collaborate. It thus makes sense to manage your activities beyond the letter of the law to create a reputation as a strong partner.

for itself the returns from those resources. Alternatively, the partner might be unwilling to sell through a contract if it believes that other transactional options will provide higher benefits to stakeholders. The seller may only be willing to sell its resources bundled with the entire company—even when the desired resource could easily be separated out. During the summer of 2011, Google's offer to license Motorola's handset patent portfolio evolved into a takeover of the entire business unit, Motorola's Mobility. This was partly because of pressure from Motorola's activist shareholders, who expected greater immediate returns from the acquisition than they would have gained from licenses.

Despite real frictions possible in licensing, firms often overestimate how much resistance will arise, and they consequently miss opportunities to use licenses effectively. Some firms overcome market frictions by systematically scanning and evaluating external resources and partners, building ties with potential providers over time as the resources develop. In established firms such as Intel, Cisco, and AstraZeneca, a specified arm of the corporation does the scanning. When a business systematically scans external resource environments, it helps grow the pool of viable partners, thereby expanding horizons. It also better understands how much support would be needed to carry out resource transfers. Such insights can then be baked into contractual arrangements. (In concert with resource scanning, we recommend that resource-seeking firms enhance their internal competences in targeted resource areas. Higher confidence in basic knowledge can help overcome—or avoid—contractual frictions.)

Moreover, even basic contracts can be adjusted when unexpected problems arise. For instance, Canadair licensed the F-86 Sabre from North American Aviation and the P-80/T-33 from Lockheed in the 1950s. Although Canadair struggled at first to use the technology, it drew on licensors' expertise and its own in-house skills and ultimately developed highly successful commercial projects.

Misinterpreting Prior Failures

Finally, executives sometimes develop blind spots about contracts when firms use this mode under the wrong circumstances. Once failure ensues, they learn the wrong lesson. Rather than recognize that failure resulted from an unsuitable pathway, they become reluctant to use basic contracts at all. The rational solution is, of course, to learn when to use contracts and when to avoid them, not categorically rule out a potentially valuable sourcing mode.

Certainly, critical problems can occur when firms attempt to use basic contracts in conditions better suited to an alliance. One of our research projects found that aerospace firms that rely on licensing for complicated new projects commonly suffer in the future, when they try to develop follow-on projects internally. This is because they lack full knowledge of the underlying technology, which was not subject to the license agreement. Similarly, pharmaceutical companies have difficulty building on licensed products—which could serve as platforms for widespread ongoing development—when the firms lack sufficient in-house expertise to evaluate the products' underlying molecular structure. In another instance, the Ford Motor Company suffered a mismatch between the design of its early sport-utility vehicles and the Firestone tires that it licensed for those SUVs during the 1990s. The mismatch affected vehicle stability, contributing to several rollover accidents. A tighter alliance between the companies would have made the SUVs and the tires more compatible.

Nonetheless, it is easy to overstate the potential problems of contracts and underestimate the costs of more complicated, external relationships. Do not blindly discard a perfectly viable option. Weigh carefully whether the resources you need are tradable through contractual arrangements or require more complex modes. Figure 3-1 outlines the key steps in this decision.

FIGURE 3-1

Basic contract versus alliance

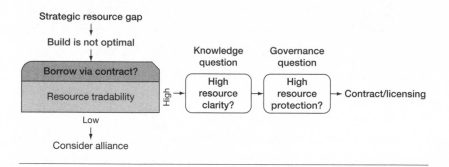

Are the Targeted Resources Tradable?

Companies that obtain resources via contractual arrangements assume that they can trade the targeted resources effectively. The critical task is to assess how tradable the targeted resources are. Tradability means that you can clearly define what you need and determine that a contract will protect the value of each partner's resources. For instance, established pharmaceutical firms commonly negotiate geographic licenses for drugs that have completed clinical trials, allowing other companies to sell the drugs in countries where the drug developer does not operate. The resources are tradable in such cases because the technical characteristics are well understood, the market boundaries are clearly defined, the terms of selling and using the drugs are clear, and potential market sizes and relevant royalty rates can be projected accurately. If the parties are confident that they understand the drugs' current and future value, then they have achieved high resource clarity and have a reasonable chance of protecting the value of their resources. If both conditions are met, the resources are tradable.

Determining tradability is not an exact science. Companies often focus narrowly on the resources, paying little attention to the relationships with the provider needed to support resource transfer. A contractual arrangement such as a license is seldom purely passive; it typically requires mutual understanding and adaptation over time as conditions change. Different firms may face different problems when negotiating for the use of seemingly similar resources. A firm knowledgeable about the targeted resource area or with strong contracting experience will face fewer obstacles than firms with less knowledge or contracting experience.

Knowledge Question: Can You Define the Targeted Resources Clearly?

Basic contracts work well when you can define targeted resources clearly. The parties involved must have a shared understanding of three elements: the current nature of the resources, the future value of the resources, and the type of working relationship needed to exchange the resources. Such resource clarity allows partners to craft a transparent agreement and manage it effectively.

The current nature of the targeted resources

Contracts work well for patents and other proprietary rights when there is resource clarity. For example, pharmaceutical firms frequently in-license and out-license the right to sell drugs for specific therapeutic purposes and in defined geographies. When Bristol-Myers Squibb wanted to enter the market for statins, it licensed from the Japanese firm Sankyo the right to sell Pravachol in the United States. The product had achieved clinical success, the market was clearly defined in both scope and size, and there were clear property rights to the chemical entity. Together, these conditions made the resource tradable. It was a straightforward matter for the firms to negotiate a multiyear sales contract.

Not all patents can be so clearly formalized. In telecommunications, a patent is not necessarily a clearly defined property right. A smartphone, for example, is a bundle of IT-combining hardware and software for sending and receiving voice, data, and video. Such complexity requires active coordination of development activities and is susceptible to thousands of potential patent claims.

Barriers to resource clarity can arise when one party knows more than the other about the value of a given resource. For instance, a particular drug may have idiosyncrasies that affect the design and cost of clinical trials. A firm that has developed the base technology underlying a patent knows far more about the technology than do potential partners, which are at a relative disadvantage and may consequently be reluctant to negotiate a contract. Bosch, the German automotive and industrial technology company, considered using a basic contract to obtain air-conditioning technology from the Japanese firm Denso, but decided not to because of Denso's far deeper knowledge of the value of the targeted resources. Wide gaps in knowledge are most commonly found with specialized resources and less commonly with more familiar ones—or those with which both parties have comparable experience.

The future value of the targeted resources

The value of resources is never static, rising and falling under the influence of a host of factors. Contracts work best with a shared understanding of the resources' *future* value. An agreement needs to provide terms for payment streams, termination rights, and other eventualities. When the future value of the new resources is elusive, often because market or technical evolution is highly uncertain, the parties will struggle, first, to agree on terms and, later, to enforce them to both parties' satisfaction. Under high uncertainty like this, contract terms can be ambiguous.

Uncertainties of this type arise in many contexts. The former Swedish drug company Astra and Merck explored a simple license to introduce Astra's anti-ulcer drug Prilosec in the United States. Both parties quickly realized how complicated that arrangement would be, requiring extended clinical tests and a new pharmaceutical marketing model for the United States. Recognizing the difficulty of distilling the various uncertainties into a dollar amount for a license, the firms created an alliance instead. Similarly, the ongoing evolution of health-care insurance in emerging markets is highly uncertain. Insurers from the developed world and emerging markets alike have found it difficult, if not impossible, to project the terms of a simple agreement to integrate across their markets. So far, they have only managed to negotiate extremely short-term contracts. And in the early 2000s, Whirlpool and the Chinese firm Haier failed to negotiate licenses to expand in each other's markets because it was hard to predict the course of market evolution. Whirlpool ended up expanding in China through an alliance with the Chinese firm Hisense-Kelon.

The working relationship with the resource partner

Difficulties over terms can arise when the exchange and integration of targeted resources requires extensive coordination between the parties. Many telecom executives we interviewed stressed that they avoid basic contracts when the buyer has *an ongoing need to work closely with a partner*. Under such circumstances, two-thirds of the executives opted for an alliance or an acquisition, depending on the level of collaboration needed. Complex learning arises wherever knowledge transfer between two parties requires shoulder-to-shoulder work among personnel, sharing information on an ongoing basis, and coordination with multiple functions at the firms such as product development and marketing.

It's important, therefore, to identify the kind of working relationship you need with your resource partner and to ask yourself multiple questions:

- Should the contract specify only resource or technology transfer, or will you need complementary marketing or support assistance?

- After negotiating a contract, can you stay up-to-date on your own, or will you need ongoing help from the supplier?

- Do you have relevant internal people to interact with the partner and ensure effective knowledge transfer? Or—if the resource lies outside your current knowledge base—will you need external experts to assist in resource transfer?

- Do you have available bandwidth (time and people) to compile information that will help the resource partner conduct an effective transfer?

- Can you cope with the added costs and potential frictions that can arise when key stakeholders are geographically dispersed?

The closer the targeted resources are to your existing knowledge base, the easier it will be to define the resources, their future value, and the kind of working relationship you will need to support their transfer. This understanding will enhance your legitimacy as a contractual partner. As one senior telecom executive put it, "to successfully source technology on the open market, you need to reach a minimum threshold of internal competencies in order to be an effective and attractive buyer."

Once the target resources have been identified, vetted, and valued—and the contract is signed—you must also draw on internal knowledge to ensure that your firm's further dealings with the resource provider fit well with your current organization.

Governance Question: Can You Protect the Resources' Value?

Resource clarity is not, in itself, enough to support a basic contract. You must also protect the value of the resources involved in the interaction—your own as well as those you contract to obtain. A contract can specify terms concerning patents and copyrights over any current and future resources that stem from the current agreement; determine shares of current and future revenue streams; identify termination conditions; and address many other factors related to using the target resources. In practice, however, such legal mechanisms are often ineffectual. Partner opportunism, resource leakage, and poor contract execution skills can imperil both sides of the agreement.

Partner opportunism

Contracts work well only when the parties enforce their contractual rights. Meaningful value protection requires three conditions: clarity, trust, and law—to wit, clear resource definition; trustworthy partners, who will deal in good faith and not take unfair advantage when opportunities arise unexpectedly; and legal safeguards that enable effective arbitration when disputes erupt over contract terms.

No matter how much effort you put into crafting the terms, no contract can fully specify all future contingencies. As one person who regularly negotiates and manages contracts told us, "all contracts are incomplete." And when firms expand in emerging markets, where—despite growing transparency—legal institutions have varying robustness, legal recourse for contractual problems is often not possible. For example, the court system in India is slow, often taking many years to adjudicate contractual disputes. This creates a disincentive to negotiate contracts there in the first place.

Both seller and buyer require protection. The seller wants to protect the value of the resources or knowledge it will transfer to the buyer. Without that protection, the seller may either refuse to contract or demand so high a price that the deal makes no sense. And for the buyer, value extends beyond the transfer of contracted resources to include a support team from the seller to assist in the resource transfer. This procedure often requires the buyer to reveal strategically important parts of its business. Without strong protection of resource value, buyers will be reluctant to contract.

These concerns arise in many industries. Some executives report they commonly face patent and intellectual-property rights issues when attempting to buy off-the-shelf technology. Many fear being unable to control intangible aspects of technology exchange; the lack of control may then cause them to become reliant on the technology provider. A telecommunications executive told us, "When we buy a technology off the shelf, we work hard on the patent issues. We need to control the technology. We need to have intellectual property rights." This requirement for detailed property rights may lead to higher contractual prices, but may provide greater control over future revenue streams.

Beyond basic intellectual property rights, licensing out a technology—especially one in an early development stage—can leave the provider exposed if a licensee fails to create new products.

The ultimate success of the licensor—its business prospects, future value, and reputation—could depend mightily on whether the buyer successfully develops the licensed technology. A licensor therefore wants assurances that the licensee is making the necessary investments and proceeding energetically to exploit the resource. Biotech firms frequently sell their drugs at a very early stage. In doing so, they hitch their hopes to the deep resources and skills of big pharmaceutical firms to carry the drugs forward to regulatory approval. But if a pharmaceutical firm loses interest and underinvests in a drug-development project, the licensed drug will likely fail—with negative consequences for the licensor. This is all the more damaging when the drug in question represents a substantial portion of the licensor's projects.

Resource leakage

In addition to the risk of being fleeced by a partner during a contractual exchange, many executives we interviewed worried that a partner could capture some of their valuable intellectual property if the exchange took place without sufficient control. One executive alluded to his firm's deep fear that once the contract ended, a resource provider would poach the firm's customers and become a competitor.

Selling partners have similar concerns. To wit, increasingly knowledgeable buyers could absorb the needed capabilities, thereby reducing the seller's value in future exchanges. One technology seller told us he is reluctant to provide detailed manuals, because he wants the buyers to need his skills and knowledge. And in the aerospace industry, some subcontractors of the originating licensor declined to reveal details of their technology to a licensee. Such reticence discourages would-be licensees and diminishes the resource-contract marketplace.

Similarly, independent sellers may refuse to customize their products. For instance, some potential suppliers of telecom services in South Africa have been unwilling to create dedicated software for telecom companies such as MTN, because they fear being unable to recoup the long-term costs of creating and refining the software.

Contract execution skills

Finally, you need to assess your ability to execute the contracting process for the targeted resource. One consideration is the availability of legal skills. For smaller firms, this typically means employing outside attorneys. Larger firms often have strong in-house legal departments with relevant skills in the targeted area. But even large firms must sometimes hire outside counsel when a contract falls outside their traditional expertise. Likewise, firms may need to bring in consultants—first to help build trusting relationships with partners in different institutional environments and later to help manage knowledge flows involving technical assistance, management needs, and cross-cultural understanding over the life of a contract.

Weak contract execution skills can be deadly, leading both to damaged relationships during negotiations and to weak terms, the negative effect of which is felt as the contract plays out over time. You cannot simply assume that knowledge will flow effectively during the life of the contract. Failure to establish knowledge-management procedures *tailored to the specific relationship* up front could easily curtail knowledge transfer. Your legal team must therefore possess adequate insight about the resource domain; only then can it craft a contract that anticipates potential transfer or relationship problems. This is all the more crucial when dealing with a resource partner with whom you have no prior working relationship.

The more your firm needs to learn from its partner, the stronger the relationship must be—not just between your personnel and the partner's, but also among your own people. In our telecom study, 55 percent of respondents reported that their firms faced substantial internal frictions integrating external with existing capabilities: staff resisted the new resources because they were "not invented here."

Another barrier to success can arise if your partner has little or no track record with licensing or lacks relevant people to assist in the resource transfer. You need to make certain, going in, that you can get sufficient attention from your supplier's *appropriately skilled* personnel. If you need significant support—and have no prior experience with a partner whose licensing track record is slight—you might want to reconsider whether a license is really the best path. If you or your partner lacks relevant contract execution skills, it often makes sense to search for external opportunities that rely less on the terms and conditions of a basic contract.

Implications for Your Resource Sourcing Strategy

Figure 3-2 summarizes the contract branch of the resource pathways framework. Answering the knowledge and governance questions will help you determine whether to consider a contract or the more complex options of alliances and acquisitions to obtain your targeted resources.

The figure highlights four combinations of resource clarity and protection, which effectively constitute a resource's tradability. These four levels of tradability suggest the four sourcing options described below. Like the internal-development pathway in chapter 2, the

FIGURE 3-2

Resource tradability and resource sourcing options

		Governance question: resource protection?	
		High	Low
	High	Resource tradability: high *Modular agreements* Contract	Resource tradability: partial *Undefended agreements* Consider alliance *Alternative*: consider complex contract
Knowledge question: resource clarity?	Low	Resource tradability: partial *Interwoven agreements* Consider alliance *Alternative*: consider complex contract	Resource tradability: low *Combination-demanding agreements* Consider alliance

options at the upper left and lower right panels are more straightforward than those at the upper right and lower left.

Modular agreements

Contracting is most appropriate when you have clarity about resource
value and the required supporting relationships and when neither partner enters unprotected into contractual arrangements. We refer to cases
in which both resource clarity and value protection are high as *modular
agreements*. In practice, modular agreements are common. For example,
over the past two decades, Eli Lilly has secured more than two hundred
licensing agreements comprising contracts that confer rights to compounds, products, delivery technologies and devices, development and
production processes, software, and geographic markets.

Combination-demanding agreements

Writing meaningful contracts to govern arm's-length exchanges may
be impossible when it is difficult to describe and to protect current or
future resources. In such cases, alliances or other, more complicated
interorganizational relationships are almost always the better option
for obtaining targeted resources. Otherwise, proceed at your own risk!
For example, in 2007, Raytheon's legal office formed a contract-based
partnership with five other companies to develop an IT system for
border inspections in the United Kingdom. The £650 million Trusted
Borders project involved extensive technical uncertainty as well as
open-ended commitments by the partners. Over the next three years,
the project encountered substantial coordination problems and failed
to produce a viable product. The British government finally sus-
pended the project in 2010.

Undefended agreements

When—despite high resource clarity—there are only limited ways to
protect resource value, basic contracts often fail. Even apparently
trustworthy partners may, over the length of a contract, face new

demands and opportunities that cause them to reinterpret the terms. This is especially a risk when the terms of a deal are difficult to enforce or when new personnel do not clearly understand the terms. For example, several US online service companies have backed out of deals that their software providers believed were long-term commitments only to discover, unhappily, that ambiguous language left substantial room for reinterpretation.

Historically, many Western multinationals operating in China, India, and other emerging markets have signed contracts with local firms and encountered resource-protection problems. Although the resources involved were clearly defined and had value that was specifically protected in the contracts, some resources unexpectedly found their way to affiliates of the local partners—and were thus beyond the enforceable scope of the contract and the control of the licensor.

When such breaches occur, efforts to arbitrate in local courts often fail or else take so long as to be useless. As noted, while these concerns continue to be real, the growing commercial strength of many emerging markets has led to greater interest in legal proprietary protection. Hence, contracts with local firms in emerging markets need case-by-case assessment of resource protection.

When resource protection is a high priority and a basic contract would leave you undefended, consider an alliance or acquisition. Before doing so, however, you may want to look into *complex contracts*, a more stringent contracting option.

Complex contracts specify contingencies that may arise during the life of a contact. These contracts typically include *hostage terms*, provisions whereby partners suffer damaging consequences if they intentionally cheat or unintentionally underperform. Hostage terms range from penalty clauses to cross-equity investments and collateral market agreements that require the parties to invest in one another. The latter two mechanisms are potent good-faith incentives since what harms one party also harms the other. Equity investments, common forms of hostage terms because equity creates a right to the residual income of a business, may be appropriate for parties whose contributions are hardest to measure.

The CME Group (which owns the Chicago Mercantile Exchange) and the Brazilian Mercantile & Futures Exchange provide an example of a hostage contract. The companies made cross-equity investments of about 10 percent in each other when they began to comarket their commodities exchange products in 2007. Even though the development activity was relatively clear, both parties were concerned about their inability to precisely specify ownership rights to the products they were developing. Similarly, Cisco often takes a minority equity position in many of its alliances both to guard against opportunistic behavior by partners and to provide rights to help coordinate ongoing development and resource transfer activities.

Interwoven agreements

When property rights are clear but the partners' resources link together in complex ways, interwoven agreements often arise. Despite their ability to protect the resources, basic contracts provide only limited guidance for resource exchange. More complex situations commonly arise with codevelopment activities in which two or more firms contribute clearly defined resources that can be combined in the creation of a new product—for instance, a new drug or a piece of software. The characteristics of the new product (and its underlying technologies) are not initially obvious, but eventually unfold during codevelopment. It is therefore difficult to write a basic contract that will govern an arm's-length exchange when the parties cannot anticipate how the resources will evolve.

Interwoven projects commonly trigger alliances or acquisitions rather than basic contracts, typically providing more effective means of obtaining the underlying resources and managing their ongoing use in new products. For example, Siemens initially considered licensing the rights to the digital technology it needed to expand in the telecom industry. It soon concluded that it understood neither the technology nor the market opportunity well enough to negotiate a clear contract with the small firms that had the needed resources. Although Siemens knew that it could have protected itself contractually—if only because it was so much larger than its would-be partners—it doubted its ability to effectively manage technology flow using basic contracts. Therefore, Siemens instead acquired several small digital technology firms to freely participate in codevelopment and market experimentation as applications and further advances in the new technology unfolded over time.

Before immediately considering alliances and acquisitions in interwoven cases, though, evaluate whether complex contracts can specify key contingencies as a way of correcting for the lack of resource clarity. Complex contracts can sometimes identify contingencies relating to unpredictable resource-development issues. Contract terms can then link to future conditions that would affect resource value or market viability. For example, the contract might provide for multiple milestone payments as uncertain future values are clarified. Such terms are common in pharmaceutical licensing, development agreements for application-specific integrated circuits (ASICs), and entertainment industry development projects. For example, when a novel is optioned to be made into a movie, the deal is typically structured to provide escalating payments to the author, as a series of specified milestones bring the project closer to production. In reality, though, the course of such projects is hard to predict, and relatively few optioned books ever reach production.

Complex contracts—whether specifying hostage terms for undefended agreements or key contingencies for interwoven relationships—offer neither perfect protection nor full knowledge clarity, even in the best of cases. Yet when partners have the basis for knowledgeable and trusting relationships, such contracts can sometimes bring stalled contracts back to life.

At the same time, complex contracts require strong contracting skills suited to the specific resource context. You need to be able to identify and negotiate appropriate terms for a particular relationship. Even more importantly, you must monitor the relationship after signing the contract, both to ensure that you and your partner are following the terms and, where reasonable, to modify the terms as unexpected events occur.

Assessment Tool and Summary

The questions in table 3-1 will help you decide when—and when not—to use basic contracts to obtain targeted resources. If most of your responses are yes, your targeted resources can be clearly defined and successfully protected through contractual agreements. If, however, most of your responses are no, you should consider other external sourcing options such as alliances or acquisitions. Of course, you might also decide to supplement contractual arrangements with partnerships or take some equity in a bid to more securely align partners' interests.

Basic contracts are a valuable complement to internal development and other sourcing modes. However, firms that seek to use contracts as a way of quickly integrating unfamiliar technologies and markets will often fare best by combining sourcing modes. For example, the glass-fiber producer Owens Corning used a mix of internal technology and licensed skills as the basis for the innovative materials it sells to producers of wind-turbine blades. In our telecom study, 62 percent of firms that acquired new resources through basic contracts also hired people with resource-relevant backgrounds. The firms thus used contracts to bootstrap internal skills.

Although contracts carry significant risks when used in the wrong situations, they are powerful tools when you can achieve both resource clarity and protection. Borrowed resources—whether obtained via contract employees, licenses, leased resources from outside contractors, or other types of basic contracts—offer a rapid on-ramp to new markets and technologies. Their effectiveness is amplified further by

TABLE 3-1

Resource tradability

Knowledge question: resource clarity		No	Yes
Nature of resources	Can we clearly define the characteristics of the resources we need?		
	Can we separate the targeted resources from their organizational context?		
Future resource value	Can we accurately define the future value of the resources?		
Supporting relationship	Do we need only limited assistance and learning from our partner?		
Knowledge distance	Do we have internal skills and knowledge in the targeted resource area?		
Governance question: resource protection			
Partner opportunism	Can we trust a potential partner to act fairly when unexpected events occur?		
	Will the relevant legal system protect our interests in case of a conflict with our partner?		
Resource leakage	Can we prevent a partner from learning proprietary knowledge that we want to avoid leaking during the contract?		
	Could a potential partner protect knowledge that it wants to avoid leaking to us during the contract?		
Contract execution skills	Do we and our partner have strong skills and relevant internal people to manage the contractual relationship?		

Answer each question about the clarity and potential protection of the targeted resources. If most of your responses are yes, consider contractual agreements (*borrow* mode). If most of your responses are no, consider other external sourcing options such as alliances or acquisitions.

shedding the costs associated with carrying underproductive employees and assets. In volatile environments, arm's-length agreements often give firms the flexibility to expand and contract quickly when circumstances and resource requirements change.

When to Borrow via Alliance
Alliance Versus Acquisition

When an arm's-length contract will not meet your resource needs, you should consider a more complex external relationship. This chapter focuses on deciding between an alliance and a full-scale acquisition. Alliances can take many forms, ranging from relatively straightforward (R&D and marketing partnerships) to potentially quite complex (freestanding joint ventures). Consequently, the agreements that govern alliances span a similar spectrum of complexity, at the high end encompassing multistage contracts, cross-investments, and complicated rights arrangements. However, all alliances involve ongoing interactions in which independent parties commit resources to a joint activity for a certain period of time.

Contracts, in their simplest form, transfer resources in one direction: from a provider to the recipient. Alliances, on the other hand, typically enable highly collaborative combinations of resources and activities by multiple parties. Ideally, they produce benefits for all participants. For example, nearly twenty-five years ago, a consortium of Wall Street firms—ardent competitors for most purposes—agreed to jointly develop what would become the industry's first shared network for electronic trading. That alliance promised to create a resource of such extraordinary value to all the participants that they transcended rivalry to achieve it. A basic contract among the firms would not have allowed enough coordination to create the innovative trading network.

Alliances can thus be negotiated between direct competitors, complementary firms, and other organizations—such as government agencies, academic institutions, technology developers, and service providers. Through alliances, firms can share risks in uncertain markets; help protect the participants' respective proprietary rights; and facilitate their ongoing, often complex interactions within an orderly framework. Although an alliance risks exposing your knowledge base to a partner, active collaboration often affords greater security than an arm's-length agreement by offering a wider range of more explicit protections and incentive-alignment mechanisms (as described for contracts in chapter 3). Alliances are most effective when relatively few people and organizational units from each party must work together on joint activities—which may also make it easier to align partners' incentives.

By contrast, if obtaining and developing strategic resources requires intense joint interactions, you will usually benefit by considering acquisition, which allows you to obtain resources *and* retain the value of your success in exploiting those resources. Again, our message about acquisitions is simple: because M&A is the most complex sourcing option, reserve it for cases where having full ownership of the resource provider really pays.

Alliances create a paradox. On the one hand, they are attractive because they are cheaper and more flexible than acquisitions. Indeed, alliances are often touted as a low-risk way to fill an emerging resource gap or access capabilities in remote geographic markets where a firm lacks familiarity. On the other hand, executives often worry especially about stoking any current competitive overlap between the parties into a full-blown future rivalry. For that reason, many executives avoid alliances. And as noted earlier, a reluctance to use them (or any other particular mode) can become entrenched and reflexive when a firm has experienced a past alliance failure that it wrongly attributes to the limitations of the mode itself.

Adding to the paradox of alliances, the usual transiency of the relationships is both an advantage and a disadvantage. For the duration of an alliance, the participating firms enjoy (albeit in a limited way) the resource-enhancing benefits of acquisition, but without the long-term entanglements, liabilities, and commitments of outright ownership. Nevertheless, transient relationships can also engender various kinds of abuse and bad faith, whose damage cannot necessarily be controlled by the terms of an agreement. A party might not realize that damage has been done until well after the alliance has ended.

Thus an alliance necessarily requires a degree of trust among the participants. But trust alone is insufficient to ensure full compliance. As Ronald Reagan famously said of a missile treaty with the Soviets: "Trust, but verify." Though business alliances rarely involve missiles, they nonetheless demand vigilance. An alliance needs active management throughout its life cycle, supported by prescient structures that set forth incentives, milestones, and termination arrangements.

Not surprisingly, alliances often turn out to be more complex than participants expected. The emerging complexity makes them tricky to manage successfully over time. Some analysts suggest that in terms of meeting partners' goals, the success rate for alliances is less than half. Fully 80 percent of the executives we surveyed expressed concerns about exclusivity, control, and resource protection in alliances. More than two-thirds reported choosing M&A over alliances when they wanted to protect their differentiation and unique resources. Many executives from established telecommunication firms view alliances in highly negative terms. One leader called them a flawed approach that would lead to "shopping core competences rather than sharing knowledge." A manager in a leading European telecom firm told us, "People often think, 'These guys are going behind our back. We're letting a competitor enter our business.'"

Blind Spots: Why Are Executives Suspicious of Alliances?

Alliances are not always appropriate, but many firms are suspicious of alliances for the wrong reasons. A dogmatic refusal to share payoffs and control lies at the root of the problem.

Reluctance to Share the Payoff

Firms sometimes avoid alliances because they do not want to share the fruits of their business activities. A publishing executive once told us why he had mixed feelings about alliances: "Joint ventures reduce the risk [of developing resources needed for new services], but also the payback." There are two problems with this view. First, alliances are not inherently less risky than other sourcing modes. Second, the shared payback for a great success, arising from allied firms' joint exertions, is far better than a full share of the minimal fruits of a failure caused by selecting the wrong sourcing mode. In other words, half a loaf is better than none at all.

To be sure, sometimes the cost of an alliance exceeds the value of the opportunity it was created to pursue—in which case it should be renegotiated or abandoned. Other times, the opportunity is so strategically valuable to one party that the needed resources must be controlled and protected through an acquisition.

Reluctance to Share Control

Many people within a firm—including senior executives, corporate development staff, and operating leaders—will strongly resist an alliance because they fear the loss of both corporate strategic control and their own personal power. Others will be reluctant to "give up" resources to outsiders, thereby failing to recognize that their firms often need to work with high-quality third parties to create leading-edge resources in the first place.

During close collaboration between alliance partners, concerns about competitive overlap may intensify. Many executives find it simply counterintuitive to willingly expose core capabilities to an outsider, thereby risking a "learning race" between the partners. Executives we have interviewed—particularly those with limited alliance experience—are frequently reluctant to open their doors at all. Only 30 percent of surveyed telecom firms believed that they had absorbed new capabilities from their alliance partners, and only 18 percent encouraged job rotation and information sharing with their alliance partners.

Executives who fear losing control in alliances are especially reluctant when the relationships involve their core domains. Because the transience of alliances might cause resource leakage, you might conclude that they are suitable only for obtaining noncore resources. However, consider a broader, more nuanced view of alliance opportunities. They can be an effective means of developing highly strategic resources, especially when you ally with world-class partners whose resources you could not develop yourself or obtain elsewhere. Moreover, the strategic value of resources can shift suddenly in a rapidly changing environment—and it is assuredly not a viable strategy to control all the entities capable of developing resources that might someday become strategic to you.

Of course, at some point, the leadership of a company must firmly assert the importance of its strategy. If an alliance is the right way forward, management will need to combine carrots and sticks to allay people's biases and fears. If you have aligned your search for needed resources with overall enterprise strategy, it will be easier to invoke the support of leadership.

Whether engendered through a history of failed alliances or by a strong, intrinsic desire to retain control, these attitudes can lead firms to avoid potentially valuable alliances. Many firms in South and Southeast Asia and sub-Saharan Africa, for instance, resist partnerships because they fear losing control of their limited resources—including skilled personnel, customers, political relationships, supply chains, and other often-scarce key assets.

Paradoxically, fears about losing control in alliances are especially strong in resource-limited environments like emerging markets, where partnerships would be particularly valuable for creating new resources. Where they have occurred, carefully targeted alliances have created considerable value. For example, a South African telecommunications company and a bank—MTN Cellular and Standard Bank—overcame their reluctance and created a powerful partnership that developed the MTN Money service, which allows customers to transfer funds using their cell phones. The partnership created a strategic win for both allies, expanding the scope of their markets and services.

The rest of this chapter will help you use the resource pathways framework to decide whether to obtain a given resource through an alliance or an acquisition. As figure 4-1 illustrates, the key question in deciding when to use an alliance is *not* whether the targeted resource is strategic or general; it is whether the activities you undertake with a partner will be sufficiently focused and compatible with each partner's goals. If they are, you will create, and retain the value of, a greater success than you would have on your own—except through an outright acquisition.

FIGURE 4-1

Alliance versus acquisition

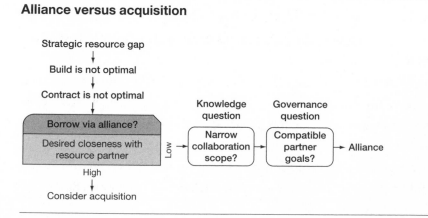

How Close Must You Be with Your Resource Partner?

When choosing between an alliance and an acquisition, you need to assess the extent of your partner's necessary involvement in the collaboration. If your partner will be deeply involved, then you will probably need substantial control—quite possibly achievable only through an acquisition. If, however, you expect a more tightly focused and limited collaboration, consider an alliance. Collaboration is *narrowly focused* when it involves a limited span of activities and simple patterns of coordination.

The need for extensive partner involvement is lower when the scope of the collaboration is focused and when your partner's goals are compatible with yours. Conversely, you will need a much greater degree of involvement from your partner when the scope of the collaboration is broad or when you and your partner's goals do not align. The need for deep partner involvement also increases the need for integration; in such cases, you should strongly consider M&A rather than alliance.

Knowledge Question: How Focused Is the Scope of the Collaboration?

An alliance has the greatest chance of success when it is narrowly focused. As the scope broadens, you will be less likely to reap the benefits of an alliance. Alliance coordination costs rise with the scope of the collaboration and tend to be substantial. In our telecom study, for instance, 65 percent of the executives involved in alliances reported high costs and coordination tensions with their partners. Firms were most likely to succeed in their collaboration strategies when they reduced the potential for coordination tensions by using alliances only for focused collaboration.

Limited span of activities

An alliance will be manageable if it spans a limited number of the parties' functions and activities (for example, only a subset of R&D, production, marketing, and regulatory staff) and involves only a few people within each given function. Limiting the points of contact helps you control the alliance's direct and indirect costs, by avoiding duplicative investments in R&D, plants, staff, and coordination activities. Even though you cannot reliably predict the outcome of an alliance, collaboration is well worth considering if you can define precisely the areas of cooperation. Many drug companies now outsource focused aspects of their clinical trials and production in collaborative relationships with third-party research and manufacturing organizations.

But if an alliance involves many components of the partner organizations, collaboration costs can rise enough to make acquisition the better alternative—notwithstanding its costs—because of the resource control and protection you gain over complex and strategically important resource development projects. For example, drugs that involve multiple indications and treatments can be extremely complicated to produce. That makes them more risky to outsource, because of the high costs of collaboration (to say nothing of the exposure of proprietary knowledge). Therefore, a drug company that lacks the internal capability for producing such drugs might benefit from acquiring a specialized producer.

Simple patterns of coordination

Alliances that are simple to coordinate are easier to manage. Some alliances are structured as *vertical supply agreements*, with one partner in charge, say, of R&D and the other in charge of commercialization. Under that model, resources are coordinated sequentially: one partner's output is input for the other partner's activity. Thus, the partners specialize in their respective distinct tasks, making coordination simple and sometimes requiring only a transfer price. In this type of alliance, each partner accesses the other's resources, but without the full transfer of any partner's knowledge to another. For instance, GE and the French firm Snecma have maintained a remarkably long-lived aircraft-engine joint venture, called CFM, since 1974. The CFM alliance rests largely on independent activities by the two partners.

Because both engage in distinct and highly specialized actions, their joint venture requires only limited contact to coordinate technical and marketing activities in different geographic areas.

Governance Question: Are Your Goals Compatible with Your Partner's Goals?

The second matter to consider is whether you and a potential partner have compatible goals. When it comes to governing an alliance, cooperation, competition, and eventual termination are all critical challenges. An alliance is quite likely doomed if partners fail to align their strategic goals—each seeking instead to capture the maximum possible short-term value at the partner's expense. Goals tend to be aligned when there is limited competitive overlap and when partners each contribute meaningful resources, enjoy symmetrical learning opportunities, and have the skills needed to manage an alliance throughout its life cycle.

Low competitive overlap

It is easiest to align the partners' objectives when there is low competitive overlap, under both current and foreseeable market conditions. With stronger competition, partners are forced to manage a complex, not-fully-trusting relationship that attempts to balance an oxymoron: collaborative competition.

The problem of too much overlap is that each ally tends to see the benefits that accrue to its partner as competitive encroachment. The Astra-Merck pharmaceutical joint venture we described earlier featured little competitive overlap. Astra was not seeking to expand in the United States; it wanted only to combine its product innovation with Merck's regulatory and marketing skills. And even though the Wall Street electronic trading consortium mentioned earlier was a partnership among fierce rivals, the project's shared goals put little or no proprietary value at risk. It was a rising tide to lift all boats.

But that is often not the case. Tensions that arose between Ford and Volkswagen (VW) in their Portugal-based joint venture, Autoeuropa, demonstrate what can happen when competitive overlap is high. In 1992, the automakers set up an alliance to coproduce a minivan—then an emerging segment in Europe—to be distributed under their respective brands and networks. Both partners would share up-front investments in product development and manufacturing. But selling essentially the same vehicle, in the same geographic markets under three rival brands (two of them owned by VW), generated significant frictions between the partners, chiefly around marketing and supply-chain strategies.

Because of its strong brand presence in Europe, Volkswagen gained a dominant share of the market. As tensions between the partners grew, VW took over the joint venture in 1999, becoming in effect a European supplier of minivans to Ford. Under the changed dynamic, Ford accused VW of using its ownership of the venture to disadvantage Ford's competitive interests. Indeed, VW had increased its market strength throughout the alliance.

If competitive overlap had been limited, tensions would likely have been lower. In contrast, the limited competitive overlap between Renault and Nissan—they focused on different geographies—helped those companies develop a successful alliance.

The Volkswagen and Ford example is far too common. Most alliances end, a good many of them badly. Even many extremely successful ventures end with one partner buying out the other's stake. Alignment efforts should therefore anticipate termination—winding down the alliance—and options for buying out the other partners. In many cases, as with VW and Ford, termination occurs without an orderly script, when a once-collaborative relationship turns sour.

Balanced resource contributions

Alliances tend to be most effective when every partner provides key resources. Some partnerships combine similar resources, producing economies of scale. This was the model for the Subaru-Isuzu Automotive (SIA) venture, formed in 1988 between Fuji Heavy Industries and Isuzu

Motors, to manufacture SUVs in the United States. But resource balance more often involves partners that provide highly differentiated, complementary resources. The long-lasting Samsung-Corning venture, for instance, began by combining Corning's cathode ray tube technology and Samsung's television production knowledge. This venture has evolved through multiple recombinations of Samsung's manufacturing expertise and Corning's knowledge of advanced materials in many product lines.

Likewise, an alliance will benefit from the partners' shared sense that it is an important activity. If one partner takes the alliance less seriously than does another, the former might devote insufficient effort to necessary activities. An imbalance in organization size can play into this dynamic. A larger firm may well undertake activities that compete with an alliance that the smaller firm is depending on. In 2011, for example, Amylin Pharmaceuticals sued its partner, Eli Lilly, after the latter allied with a different drug maker to codevelop a medicine that would compete with the one Amylin and Eli Lilly had comarketed.

Symmetrical learning opportunities

As noted, executives often fear that an alliance will lead to a learning race that advantages one partner at the other's expense. You need to assess this risk. Learning is often a predictable alliance outcome. But when learning is among the foreseen benefits, those opportunities must be balanced.

For example, because of an endemic imbalance in young, entrepreneurial firms' ability to learn from their larger partners, the entrepreneurs feel exploited. The smaller firm provides its established partner with leading-edge technology, but ends up stymied when it cannot access and integrate the partner's commercial, marketing, and other organizational skills—which are exactly those that an entrepreneur needs most to grow. For its part, the large firm has a far easier time capturing new technology skills from the upstart.

It is a kind of devil's bargain, looking good at first but aging badly. One of our research projects found that industry entrants often gain a quick on-ramp into the market by allying with established firms, but soon encounter barriers to further growth.

The rate at which resource partners learn and capture resources is also an issue in alliances between large companies, most notably in the context of market-entry alliances between multinational firms and local partners. The sidebar "When Harmony Turns Discordant" outlines one such example.

WHEN HARMONY TURNS DISCORDANT

The Hero Honda Joint Venture

Most alliances are based on the premise of complementary resource contribution. Typically, a firm with strong technology will seek a partner that offers access to otherwise unobtainable market knowledge, commercial resources, and customer segments. Sometimes, however—as with Japan's Honda and India's Hero—a foreign firm (in this case, Honda) will partner with a local firm to both access market knowledge and circumvent regulations that exclude foreign businesses.

Thus, an alliance can sometimes begin as a marriage of convenience, entered into by the foreign firm mainly to secure the right to compete locally. Of course, the foreign company can also pursue other purposes and deliver significant value to both parties over time. But beneath the surface, misalignments may also fester and worsen.

In 1984, Honda and Hero established a joint venture known as Hero Honda Motors Limited to manufacture two-wheeled motorbikes (the dominant form of motorized consumer transportation in India). In the years before India liberalized its business climate to welcome foreign investment, Honda needed a local partner to do business in India. The Japanese firm also wanted access to local market knowledge, a recognized local brand, manufacturing assets, and a distribution network. For its part, Hero wanted access to Honda's technology— notably its high-performing motorcycle engines—for which the two firms negotiated a technical licensing agreement. The Hero Honda alliance grew successfully and became the world's largest producer of two-wheeled vehicles.

Over the course of the alliance, however, tensions arose between the partners. Hero grew increasingly frustrated with Honda's reluctance to share its
engine technology. Although Honda provided engines to the joint venture,
Hero had expected that throughout the alliance, the Indian partner would
learn how to design and manufacture such engines for itself. But as time
passed, Hero perceived that the hoped-for collaborative learning benefits
were accruing mostly to Honda—in the form of commercial and distribution
capabilities and Indian market knowledge. The two partners disagreed about
what the agreement had promised, explicitly or implicitly, in terms of technology transfer to India. They struggled to find consensus as the partnership
evolved. Hero felt strongly disadvantaged.

When the alliance came up for renewal in the mid-1990s, Hero negotiated
tougher financial conditions on the royalties it paid for Honda's engines. But the
improved terms did little to soothe tensions about technology transfer and con-
flicting goals. Nearly a decade later, in 2004, Honda announced plans to set up its
own subsidiary, which would, of course, compete with Hero Honda products. In
the intervening years, India's economic reforms had made it easier for foreign firms
to do business there. Honda downgraded its relationship with Hero to be more
operational than strategic. Ultimately, the partners concluded that the venture had
become too complicated for an alliance. Honda began to divest its stake in 2011.

In hindsight, Honda entered the alliance with an explicit learning objective and
the intention of going it alone in India as soon as regulatory reforms would allow it
to do so. Hero also had learning objectives, but it failed to create mechanisms to
ensure that it could capture and internalize the desired knowledge from its partner. Honda protected its core technology, but was active in learning about local
distribution, supply chains, labor management, and other business processes.
Unlike Honda, Hero did not protect its proprietary knowledge. Nor did it successfully leverage its strong initial negotiating position to ensure that it could absorb
Honda's engineering expertise and create parallel internal R&D capabilities.

At the beginning, the alliance was valuable for both partners. But the initial
terms left room for the goals to become increasingly misaligned over the years.
And India's business liberalization reforms provided Honda with an irresistible
opportunity to pursue what had been its goal from the outset: to become a
knowledgeable, autonomous competitor in India's prosperous motorbike market.

Alliance execution skills

Finally, successful alliances require effective alliance execution skills. Viable allies have credible resources, can be trusted to negotiate honestly, and are likely to sustain effective relationships over the life of the alliance. To assess whether allies have these qualities means gaining genuine confidence in the collaborative commitment and chemistry of your own staff and that of your ally. You may not expect an alliance to last forever, but it must endure until you achieve your goals—sometimes, as we have seen, for decades.

In a perfect world, you would have many possible allies with which to negotiate. More often, though, there will be only a few suitable partners—perhaps even just one—that possess the resources you need. But that makes sense. After all, how many firms could right now give you rapid access to the market segments, the technologies, or the regulatory relationships that you need to expand your business? A small club, in all likelihood.

Even with a few viable options, though, you can often negotiate and build a successful partnership. This is especially true when would-be allies can see that your use of their resources might also lead them to new market segments and customer sets or might further develop a flagging asset. Potential synergy is an attractor. In such cases, your incentives and those of your partner will more easily align.

If no viable ally exists, attempting to force an alliance with a suboptimal partner will almost certainly fail, no matter how strong your alliance execution skills. You will naturally have candidates in mind when you start down the alliance pathway. In each case, you must ask the knowledge and governance questions. The answers will help you identify the most desirable characteristics of viable allies and make a good decision.

When weighing the manageability of an alliance, consider the particular backgrounds and biases of would-be partners. Firms lacking prior alliance experience might, for example, be hyperalert to signs of possible bad faith or quick to lose patience with consensus-based decision making. Inexperienced alliance partners tend to overestimate the amount of control they will exert over a partner's activities; they may therefore lose sight of the long-term value of genuine give-and-take. Likewise, firms with a history of relying on either build or buy strategies will more likely strive to get the upper hand in managing alliances—even when consensus would probably produce better results.

Alliance execution skills span a variety of activities and alliance phases. You need to be able to undertake effective pre-alliance planning. This includes prospecting for appropriate partners, accurately assessing potential resource value, negotiating clear agreements, and creating strong business plans. Once the alliance is under way, you need to clearly define numerous parties' roles; provide effective oversight; build strong ongoing relationships, both within and across the partners; manage (inevitable) conflicts; and maintain clarity about the main goal of the relationship, even as it evolves over time.

One of the critical mistakes in managing an alliance is to treat it like an internal unit of the company—an approach that often arises from the best of intentions. We vividly recall a conversation with a financial-services executive who declared, "This alliance is so important to us that we are going to treat it as if it was a subsidiary!" A year later, the same leader was deeply frustrated that his partners would not follow his direction. But alliance partners possess strategic autonomy. They have strong traditions, tendencies, and motivations that may lead their executives to ignore directives that don't align with the enterprise's internal dynamic. Thus the partner firm's executives are radically unlike managers of subsidiaries, who must follow orders if they hope to advance in their careers.

Firms that have engaged in many alliances are at risk of false déjà vu, wrongly applying past experience to the context of a new alliance. The best approach is a new slate: identify the unique, central issues that would arise in the alliance you are considering. They might be legal challenges around negotiating alliance terms; the management challenges of sharing staff and transferring knowledge, or monitoring and adjusting activities; the challenges of dealing with conflict; or the need to make ongoing gap analyses as circumstances change and the alliance evolves. If, after considering these factors, you find that you currently lack the needed execution skills for the project, then you must decide whether the opportunity justifies investing the time and money to create that base of skills. If not, then pursuing an M&A—as long as you have relevant skills for that option—may make better sense.

Also assess whether you have sufficient financial strength to sustain an alliance in the context of the particular targeted resource. Consider both the direct and the opportunity costs of pursuing the alliance's goals. Committing money to an alliance necessarily limits your ability to engage in other ventures. Although often less expensive than acquisitions, alliances sometimes require initial investments of tens or even hundreds of millions of dollars, plus commitments to additional (perhaps increasing) expenditures over time. You cannot necessarily assume that an alliance will be less expensive than a focused acquisition.

Implications for Your Resource Sourcing Strategy

Figure 4-2 summarizes the issues that arise along the collaboration stem of the resource pathways framework. Answering the knowledge and governance questions will help you decide whether to obtain resources through an alliance or an acquisition.

The figure highlights four combinations of goal compatibility and scope of collaboration, which determine how closely you align with your potential resource partner. As in earlier chapters, the options at the upper left and lower right panels are more straightforward than those at the upper right and lower left.

Focused and compatible alliances

Much like a string quartet, focused and compatible alliances involve a limited number of players who know their roles and require limited contact as they weave their parts together. The individuals collaborate

FIGURE 4-2

Desired closeness with resource partner and resource sourcing options

Governance question: partner's goal compatibility?

	High	Low
Narrow	Desired closeness with resource partner: low *Focused and compatible alliances* Alliance	Desired closeness with resource partner: medium *Focused but incompatible alliances* Consider acquisition *Alternative*: consider complex alliance
Wide	Desired closeness with resource partner: medium *Compatible but broad alliances* Consider acquisition *Alternative*: consider complex alliance	Desired closeness with resource partner: high *Integration-demanding alliances* Consider acquisition

Knowledge question: collaboration scope?

successfully without a conductor. Alliances of this type—where resource combination activities are focused and the partners' goals are compatible—make abundant sense and are often extremely successful.

Consider the alliance that we described earlier, between MTN and Standard Bank, to develop an application for cell-phone money transfers in Nigeria, Uganda, and elsewhere in Africa. The alliance required the engagement of only a few people from each of the firms to produce a substantial strategic payoff. Similarly, Kingfisher Airlines and Jet Airways in India created an alliance to combine routes in their secondary markets. The partnership—which involves coordinating scheduling and reservations—requires only a few people to manage. Air Asia in Malaysia and Virgin Airlines in the United Kingdom have created a similar focused alliance to link Air Asia's Southeast Asian routes with Virgin's long-haul routes to Australia, Europe, and the Middle East.

Even the major international airline alliances (Star Alliance, OneWorld, and SkyTeam) are sustained by highly focused interactions among the partners, executed mainly through the alignment of their respective information systems, which coordinate bookings and frequent-flyer programs. These benefits are achieved without other forms of extensive integration among the alliance members. Note that earlier contract-based initiatives between international airlines were far less effective. Because the contract model couldn't adequately support the need for members' ongoing engagement, the companies paid too little attention to issues of information system compatibility—leading to a rash of missed bookings and connections and many infuriated passengers. By comparison, today's alliance model offers substantial strategic payoff for the member airlines.

Sometimes, focused alliances can ripen into acquisitions if the partner relationship unexpectedly becomes more complex. Eli Lilly initiated an alliance with Seattle-based ICOS to develop the drug Cialis. After Cialis succeeded in the erectile-dysfunction market, the partners saw opportunities to use the drug's base chemistry to develop treatments for cancer and other medical conditions. Eli Lilly viewed these additional markets as an interrelated part of its portfolio growth and decided to acquire ICOS rather than continue the alliance. That put Eli Lilly on a much sounder footing to manage the complicated activities involved in the development and trials of the related products.

Integration-demanding alliances

These alliances are much like attempts to create music when there are many musicians, each playing a different tune at a different tempo. It is nearly impossible to create and manage a successful alliance if you require broad engagement, across multiple functions, with an ally whose incentives are markedly different from yours. In that case, acquisition will probably provide a better way of obtaining the targeted resource. The Ford-VW alliance exemplifies an integration-demanding relationship that failed. Likewise, Merrill Lynch and HSBC created a joint venture in 2000, with the goal of providing online banking and investment services for customers in the United Kingdom,

Australia, Canada, Germany, Japan, and Hong Kong. Each company provided an executive to serve as the venture's CEO and COO. However, when the demands of managing the relationship went beyond the scope of alliance governance, HSBC took over the venture in 2002. It would be easy to blame the early problems on the people who were assigned to the leadership roles, but in fact, the problems stemmed from the choice of pathway to obtain the desired resources.

Firms that enter into integration-demanding alliances often achieve greater success after moving to an acquisition. During the 2000s, Spain's Santander Bank expanded extensively in South America, targeting additional customer segments with a range of new products and services. Santander initially considered forging alliances with banks in Brazil, Argentina, and other countries in the continent. But it quickly realized that the relationships would be too complex to manage as partnerships of independent entities. (Just the challenge of aligning and orchestrating the incentives needed for each alliance would have been a tall order.) Instead, Santander acquired several South American banks and used them as focal points for designing and introducing new services.

Focused but incompatible alliances

These collaborations risk falling apart because one or more partners place disproportionate emphasis on their own incentives. Continuing the musical analogy, many successful and talented bands have failed because a lead singer or guitarist believed his or her goals were more important than the success of the band as a whole. In business relationships, alliances are difficult to manage when any partner overvalues its own agenda.

The 2011 attempt to negotiate an oil exploration alliance between British Petroleum (BP) and the Russian company Rosneft was a relatively focused alliance that failed because of misaligned incentives. In this case, BP's existing partner for energy sector activities in Russia, TNK, objected to the deal with Rosneft and used the terms of its prior deal with BP to block the new venture. BP could not find a way to bring TNK's interest in line with the new relationship. In such situations, you will often need to consider some form of acquisition to help govern your rights.

But acquisition is not necessarily a foregone conclusion in cases of misaligned incentives. You may want to consider a more *complex alliance*. While they do support higher levels of partner engagement than contracts, alliances tend to be more successful when they are less complex and thus easier to manage. Misaligned incentives are typically a red flag pointing toward acquisition. But when such an alliance features focused resources, a complex alliance might successfully address the lack of alignment between partner incentives.

Complex alliances do much the same thing that complex contracts do (see chapter 3), resolving conflicts around goals by using hostage terms and other measures to help align incentives and deter bad-faith conduct. In addition to hostage terms such as shared equity and cross-licensing deals, a complex alliance might also provide oversight mechanisms. These could include multifaceted working groups, each consisting of people from different functions at both partners. Their work would be governed by detailed agreements—spelling out, for example, conditions for gaining access to a clearly defined range of each partner's technology and markets. Complex alliances do not offer perfect protection, even in the best of cases. However, like complex contracts, they can help bring seemingly infeasible projects back to life. Alliances increasingly feature cross-equity holdings and control rights as hostages that help align incentives and thereby protect the partners' strategic interests. Such terms assure that the success or failure of alliance activities will have significant impact on each partner's short- and long-term performance.

GE negotiated a complex alliance when it entered the Japanese market for medical imaging instruments in the 1970s. At the time, it had strong functional skills but needed a much different organization to develop and sell imaging devices tailored to the Japanese market.

Believing that it could not create a viable internal unit—even a semi-autonomous one—GE allied with Yokogawa Hokushin Electric Corp., a Japanese firm well suited to the market. The two parties negotiated extensive control systems and technology transfer mechanisms, enabling innovation to flow in both directions as the partnership moved forward. GE gradually internalized what it learned through the partnership. It became a leader in the Japanese market, having mastered locally relevant organizational skills, and used product advances from Japan to compete globally.

Nonetheless, even successful complex alliances can become difficult to manage over time. Consider BP's strained relationship with TNK. Although the venture has successfully exploited oil reserves, there have been extensive, ongoing arguments among the partners about governance and strategy—including TNK's obstruction of BP's attempt to form an alliance with Rosneft to develop Arctic oil fields. These tensions created openings for competitors such as ExxonMobil, which ultimately allied with Rosneft.

The strength of your alliance-execution skills is particularly important in complex alliances. You need the ability to negotiate, monitor, and coordinate complicated terms in a dynamic environment. Complex alliances are a viable strategy for firms with substantial alliance experience, but potentially deadly to a neophyte. Therefore, be scrupulously honest in assessing your execution skills. If they don't measure up, but a complex alliance is nonetheless of vital importance, you must invest in obtaining the necessary skills.

Compatible but broad alliances

These alliances occur when partners' incentives are well aligned but collaboration requires many points of contact. In this model, the partners are similar to a symphony orchestra, with many musicians and different instruments all needing to blend their respective parts into a single, harmonic whole. Under the wide scope of collaboration in a compatible but broad alliance, business allies might struggle for strategic autonomy. If that disconnect is irresolvable, consider an acquisition. But before you jump, realize that this situation, too, may benefit from a more complex alliance that could mitigate orchestration challenges.

As the complexity of collaboration rises, alliances require more structure and control. Firms often use additional ties, such as equity arrangements, to supplement complex alliances. The international alliance between automakers Renault and Nissan is a successful complex alliance held together with substantial formal structure. The French and Japanese firms now undertake considerable operating collaboration in areas such as market development and supply-chain management. Cross-equity holdings—with Renault owning 37 percent of Nissan, and Nissan owning 15 percent of Renault—help keep incentives aligned when each firm undertakes activities that could affect its ally. The near lack of overlap in the companies' respective geographic markets further enhances alignment by allowing the firms to focus on coordinating production activities without the distraction of competitive worries.

Complex alliances that attempt to solve the challenges of either incentive misalignment or broad interparty collaboration require careful design and must secure a strong commitment from all partners. Firms sometimes attempt to structure alliances as networks of cross-company teams. These teams typically span different functions and levels of the partner organizations, pursue different types of mandates, and report to widely distributed leadership. Alliances that involve significant cross-learning goals or codevelopment activities often require networks of such teams dispersed across the companies. Successful collaboration requires a structure that facilitates pooling of the partners' resources and talents. Although a loosely coupled, informal task force might be appropriate for relatively focused activities, these more complex situations may require formal joint-venture entities to pool and coordinate resources.

A classic example of co-learning is the New United Motor Manufacturing Inc. (NUMMI) alliance between General Motors and Toyota. The two firms established NUMMI in 1984, at the site of a former GM assembly plant in Fremont, California. The purpose of the alliance was to manufacture cars to be sold by both automakers under their own brands. GM expected to use the joint venture to learn about lean manufacturing from the Japanese, while Toyota gained its first manufacturing foothold in North America and a chance to implement its production system in the US labor environment. The venture successfully produced vehicles until 2010, although most observers believed that Toyota gained more knowledge from the alliance than did its US partner. Indeed, Toyota used its increased knowledge of the US environment to collaborate in developing electric vehicles with Tesla Motors, which purchased part of the NUMMI plant in 2010.

Alliance complexity almost always creates tensions. Even if partners can agree on ownership shares and other governance conditions (over which initial disagreements are often enough to sink a complex alliance), subsequent problems commonly derail partnerships that require intense coordination. BP's experience in Russia is a case in point. If you cannot define coordination activities clearly, or if you are concerned about your ability to align incentives, then even a complex alliance might not work.

When both the span of activities is broad and the coordination needed is intense, even a complex alliance will eventually break down and may trigger an acquisition in some form. With Airbus, the European aircraft consortium, each of the four national partners initially tried to maintain its strategic autonomy. The partners allocated tasks, necessarily supporting significant duplication of activities during each round of design, because the dominant objective of each partner was to remain capable of manufacturing a full-fledged aircraft, not to create an optimal collaborative venture. The determination to preserve partner autonomy ultimately failed. Facing strong competition from Boeing, Airbus could not afford the high coordination costs of the members' insistence on autonomy. Finally, in 2001, the partners combined their activities into a formal joint stock company, EADS, effectively creating a completely new and independent organization into which the partners transferred their relevant assets.

Similarly, in 1990 Volvo and Renault created a complex partnership that both firms expected would give them greater scale in the global auto industry. However, the activities within the scope of the alliance were simply too complicated to be guided by independent collaborators. The partnership quickly fell into complicated, ineffectual efforts by each company to shape the relationship to its own ends. The alliance failed in 1994, an event seen as having caused Volvo's 1999 acquisition by Ford. Renault, for its part, gained from the failure some insight that helped the automaker structure its subsequent, more successful alliance with Nissan.

These examples reinforce our core point about alliances: they work best when exchanging knowledge and other resources requires focused engagement by partners who share compatible goals. Complex alliances can sometimes address the challenges of *extensive* coordination and *misaligned* goals—but only if the parties possess strong alliance execution skills. If coordination needs are high because many parts of the partner organizations are involved or the partners clearly have different strategic needs, then collaboration costs and difficulties usually become so high that acquisition makes more sense.

Assessment Tool and Summary

Table 4-1 outlines questions that can help you decide whether to seek an alliance with your resource partner to obtain needed resources. If most of your responses are yes, consider an alliance; the relationship you need with your partner is focused and your partner's goals are compatible with yours. However, if most of your responses are no, you should consider pursuing full control of your partner through an acquisition.

Alliances, highly effective tools for obtaining targeted resources with high strategic value, are particularly valuable when partners have a narrowly focused collaboration with compatible goals. When an arm's-length contract would be insufficient for managing the neces-

TABLE 4-1

Desired closeness with your resource partner

Knowledge question: scope of collaboration		No	Yes
Span of activities	Would collaboration involve few functions and people at our firm?		
	Would collaboration involve few functions and people at the partner's firm?		
Complexity of coordination	Would collaboration involve few points of contact between our people and the partners' people?		
	Would each partner's contributions be specialized and require only limited coordination to sustain the partnership?		
	Would the need for co-learning be limited?		
Governance question: partners' goal compatibility			
Competitive overlap	Is there little competitive overlap between our firm and our partner?		
Resource contribution	Will our firm and our partner contribute a balanced share of key resources?		
Alliance importance	Will an alliance be of similar strategic importance to our firm and our partner?		
Learning opportunities	Would an alliance provide our firm and our partner with similarly valuable learning opportunities?		
Alliance execution skills	Do both our firm and our partner have relevant skills and people to manage an alliance over time?		

Answer each question about the knowledge fit and organizational fit of the targeted resources. If most of your responses are yes, consider an alliance (*borrow* mode). If most of your responses are no, consider an acquisition.

sary relationship, an alliance can successfully support focused engagement, allowing you and a partner to create new value by digging deeply into a small set of shared resources. In circumstances that might seem to warrant an acquisition—those requiring either intense coordination or strong medicine to assure incentive alignment—*complex alliances* may provide safeguards that make an alliance viable. Ultimately, however, alliances are not appropriate when either coordination or incentive challenges cannot be satisfactorily resolved. In such cases, you must consider an acquisition.

When to Buy
Acquisition Versus Alternatives

Up to this point in our book, we have consistently warned of the costs, risks, and entangling complexities of acquisitions. The buying strategy is appropriate only when other, more straightforward and transient strategies would fall short of achieving your goals. This chapter assumes that you now find yourself at the threshold of last resort: you need more encompassing access to strategic resources than in an arm's-length contract and greater control over those resources than an alliance would allow. How should you proceed?

Begin by defining what you need an acquisition to accomplish. M&A can serve many purposes. Which combination of benefits do you require?

On the plus side, M&A is a potent leadership tool. The new leader of a resource-rich company can use an acquisition to establish a presence quickly by making a bold mark on the company. An established CEO, hoping to accelerate change within the company and catch up with a market leader, can use the buy mode to overcome inertia and achieve quick market-share gains. The leadership of a strong business unit within a firm can use M&A to maintain its competitive lead in the market.

Strategic M&A can rapidly reshape a business. The Indian automaker Tata Motors, for instance, upgraded its product development capabilities and moved toward more premium segments with three shrewdly calculated acquisitions: Korea's Daewoo Motors in 2004, Britain's Jaguar Land Rover in 2008, and the Italian design and engineering firm Trilix in 2010. The enterprise software vendor Oracle Corp., between 2009 and 2011, undertook a series of acquisitions—including Sun Microsystems and RightNow Technologies—to broaden its product line and service capabilities.

With specific resources in mind, acquisitions can help you overcome shortages of people with desirable talents, thereby bolstering organic growth. For example, the global energy industry suffers from a chronic shortage of highly qualified engineers and project managers. Consequently, British-based service-engineering firm AMEC has recently made thirty acquisitions to obtain engineering skills necessary for expanding its geographic footprint.

On the negative side, M&A failures can be expensive. In 2010, the Swiss drug maker Novartis decided to close the UK biotech company NeuTec Pharma, which Novartis had purchased in 2007 at a premium more than 100 percent higher than NeuTec's valuation. At the time, NeuTec was developing drugs to fight hospital infections. Unfortunately, nine months after the purchase, NeuTec's lead product failed to receive European regulatory approval. Given the product and regulatory uncertainties—along with the difficulties of integrating a twenty-employee target firm into a much larger group—would it have made better sense for Novartis to first enter into an alliance to codevelop drugs with NeuTec? Even when an alliance is not viable in such a case, you must still factor in uncertainties and other challenges (for example, by using payment milestones) when structuring an acquisition deal.

Executives must use acquisitions selectively and learn to walk away from deals that don't make sense. During our years of engagement with companies in many industries, we have observed a striking pattern. Firms that lack well-established corporate development activities often compensate by suddenly charging their executives with pursuing M&A to expand the company. Sometimes, of course, you can't achieve the right kind of growth in any other way. But if acquisition becomes the default solution for inadequate internal capabilities, you have a strategic governance problem on your hands. Sometimes you also have an incoherent mess.

One of our students faced an M&A challenge at a first-tier supplier in the auto industry. His company's newly appointed CEO had attended a seminar and learned that he needed to have audacious goals for transforming the company and that M&A was an effective rapid-transformation tool. The company had deep pockets at the time, so the CEO went on a buying spree. Our student, put in charge of integrating the hodgepodge that his boss had purchased, wanted our advice on how to avoid integration mistakes. We were able to help—up to a point. But in truth, the major mistake had already been made. Most of the acquisitions made little sense and fit together poorly. A year later, the parent firm was in a mess and on the market, the CEO was gone, and our student was looking for another job.

As discussed, the boundaries between alliances and M&A can blur. Over time, some alliances become M&A. Acquisitions can also become alliances, such as when a firm created via acquisition later splits into separate, cooperating units. Some target firms preserve their autonomy within an acquirer and function as independent units within their new corporate parent. As described in chapter 4, some dominant firms mistakenly treat their alliance partners like internal subsidiaries. Finally, some alliances end up providing more substantial resource benefits than does M&A.

Of course, acquisitions differ fundamentally from alliances with respect to ownership and control: an acquisition achieves a controlling interest, but an alliance does not. Hence the buy mode is superior when unified ownership and centralized control will help you exploit more combined resources than you could with an independent ally. A firm often needs more control when it wants to increase its commitment in the targeted resource area and needs deep involvement from its resource partners. Although alliances don't enable such intensive exploitation of joint assets, they are usually less costly and more flexible than acquisitions, which make them especially appealing in areas of high technological or market uncertainties.

In terms of process, acquisitions also differ from alliances. An alliance is usually negotiated between two partners with complementary aims. M&A often involve multiple bidders and can serve a more complex set of purposes, including cost savings, increased market power, and geographic market entry. For focused, clearly defined resources and objectives, alliances are your better bet.

Therefore, when nothing short of an acquisition will successfully meet your needs, choose that mode. Acquiring and integrating a target firm requires many financial and managerial resources and is thus a crude means of obtaining specific resources. The firm you acquire comes bundled with many duplicate or nonstrategic resources that you must restructure and divest. These are costly and disruptive activities. Consequently, an overreliance on acquisition adds to your overall risk, stretching your integration capabilities too thinly—potentially even to the breaking point. Indeed, one difficult alliance is usually preferable to one acquisition too many.

Acquisition consists of many steps, each with the potential either to facilitate or derail your success. The real killer, though, is postmerger integration: creating value from the blended resources of an acquisition. Even firms experienced in M&A struggle with this piece of the puzzle in every deal. Each new acquisition is endowed with a unique set of resources, people, and values. There is thus no repeatable template other than to study, learn, and plan for everything that makes *this* integration challenge different from the last. In that sense, postmerger integration is more job-shop ingenuity than assembly-line automation—though you will eventually develop a menu of repeatable best practices.

A key part of postmerger integration is your decisions on which acquired resources to keep and which to sell off. If you are not disciplined about selling off resources that have no useful place in the new organization, you risk carrying excess baggage. This is an especial risk when you make an acquisition to control a few clearly identified, high-value resources. In these cases, the acquirer may focus on rapidly exploiting the relevant resources while delaying divestments so as to avoid disrupting the existing organization and destabilizing the people who created the needed resources' value. As a result, acquirers often end up paying an acquisition premium for resources that they do not use.

On the other hand, firms can also restructure and integrate the target firm's resources too quickly, believing that they can whip a target firm into shape by getting rid of excess fat. While leveraging the target firm's core resources, they simultaneously divest and strip assets, downsize staff, and sell off parts of the business. This can become a problem when what first appeared to be fat turns out to have been muscle and bone. In a large-scale research program we conducted on 250 acquisitions in US and European manufacturing sectors during the 1990s, a target firm's resources in R&D, manufacturing, marketing, and sales were from three to five times more likely to be downsized than those of the acquirers. In the long term, such aggressiveness can lead to the loss of valuable capabilities.

You will avoid these mistakes only if you can clearly map the integration process and sustain the motivation of key people at both firms. Overly centralized control can harm cooperation between target and acquirer and destroy the value of the combined resources, yet too little control will lead to lost opportunities for value creation. If you cannot integrate properly, reconsider less integrative options, such as alliances or partial acquisitions. Let's explore why managers so often leap into deals without undertaking the kind of analysis we're talking about.

Blind Spots: Why Do Executives Jump to M&A?

One business axiom says that mergers and acquisitions often create more headlines than value. Some studies indicate that 70 percent of deals fail to achieve their objectives. While such studies may disproportionately include large deals—which are particularly difficult to negotiate and implement—high percentages of all acquisitions fail. Like many other researchers, we found that on average, acquisitions destroy value for the acquirer's shareholders. Only 27 percent of telecom executives we surveyed had successfully extracted the value of the target firm's capabilities. Many firms expect acquisitions to accelerate their growth, but executives often turn to M&A for the wrong reasons, including their own self-interest, an overcommitment to the buy mode, the allure of a particular target, and the use of M&A as a blocking strategy or a strategic shortcut.

Managerial Self-Interest

Self-interest poses serious problems in decisions about M&A. Many studies document that acquisitions feed managers' egos, reputations, and empire-building aspirations; increase their compensation and perks; mask the poor performance of their current portfolios; maintain their attractiveness for future CEO posts; or simply protect their present jobs. At the basic level of raw ambition, problems arise when executives use acquisitions unthinkingly as a shortcut to meet growth targets and generate publicity for themselves. At a deeper level, managers abuse M&A because of incentive systems that encourage them to ask the wrong questions, emphasizing size over real synergy, speed over careful due diligence, and short-term earnings per share over long-term value creation.

Managers should focus instead on how a potential acquisition will improve the company's resource advantage in ways that competitors could not easily match. To do this, they should (and largely do) weigh the firms' combined benefits by projecting future cash flows. The aim is to ensure that the purchase price is in line with projected future value. Unfortunately, as they undertake this analysis, many managers fail to consider the long-term value-creation potential of the resources to be acquired. Instead, they focus on the near term: "How will this acquisition affect our earnings per share and our growth rate? How will it help us reach market share targets? How will it affect our share price (and, of course, the value of my options)?"

Though such questions may be relevant, they often generate biased answers, because firms can achieve the targets they set by either creating or destroying value. To make sure that those objectives are achieved through creating rather than destroying value, managers must examine how the *core resources* of the acquisition—which influence share price, earnings per share, market share, growth, and customer satisfaction— contribute to lasting value. When their decisions look solely at the short term, managers can destroy value while pursuing promotions, bonuses, and other personal incentives. An especial risk arises from the tendency to benchmark CEO compensation across companies of similar size so that bigger becomes better. Consequently, some firms overpay for acquisitions because the companies are urged on by advisers more interested in seeing the transaction take place than ensuring that value is created in the process.

Overcommitment

Even leaders who do not suffer from excessive self-interest can mismanage an acquisition by becoming overcommitted—both to acquisition as a mode of growth and to the particular target that first inspired their interest. It is easy to get carried away by the dynamics underlying the acquisition. For instance, many stakeholders will push hard toward the completion of a deal. Internally, the M&A and business-development teams have been working on the deal for weeks or months and are deeply invested in it. Externally, powerful forces at investment-advisory and banking partners have financial incentives, and a strong reputational interest, to push the deal forward. Thus, the process itself often leads to an escalation of commitment, which makes it difficult for a would-be acquirer to walk away from a deal.

Boston Scientific apparently fell into this trap when it acquired the cardiovascular device company Guidant in 2006. In 2004, Johnson & Johnson (J&J) had been close to purchasing Guidant. For several months, J&J had explored the opportunity and negotiated a price of $24 billion—arrived at by assessing the value J&J believed it could create by integrating Guidant's resources and capabilities. But after concerns surfaced about Guidant's cardiac defibrillators, J&J lowered its offer to $22 billion. Once that happened, J&J rival Boston Scientific jumped in with a $25 billion offer, which it later increased to $27 billion. Given the defibrillator concerns, Johnson & Johnson walked away from the deal, believing that the new price overstated Guidant's value. Although Boston Scientific won the auction, most observers today believe that it vastly overpaid. Moreover, it has struggled to integrate Guidant's assets and hobbled its own core business in the process.

M&A deals often occur in waves. The 1990s featured consolidating deals; the mid-2000s drove equity deals that were fueled by globalization, deregulation, and booming stock markets around the world. When competitors go on a buying spree, it is hard for an individual firm to sit back and watch. Executives may have twinges of caution, but will often conclude that such contrariness will damage their reputations as bold decision makers. In a study of the fine-chemicals industry in Europe during the early 2000s, we found strong evidence of copycat behavior. Managers simply mimicked the M&A moves of competing firms and used similarly inflated acquisition multiples—undeterred by the market's negative reception of previous, comparable deals.

Blocking Strategy

Firms sometimes use acquisitions to stop competitors from purchasing a target (some of this motive was at play in Boston Scientific's pursuit of Guidant). While such efforts sometimes yield short-term payoffs, they rarely create lasting value. The buyer has to incur the costs of integrating or breaking up the target. Moreover, competitors can almost always find alternative—and sometimes superior—ways of obtaining the "blocked" resources. Nonetheless, 50 percent of surveyed telecom executives involved in M&A told us they had bought a resource provider to prevent a competitor from acquiring it.

Perceived Time Pressure

Even executives driven by a thoughtful strategic vision sometimes use acquisitions when other modes would work better. Under the pressure of time, competition, and industry consolidation, firms may see acquisitions as a rapid way of obtaining targeted resources and achieving an advantage before their rivals can. In our telecom industry study, 63 percent of surveyed firms stated that time pressures made them choose acquisitions over alliances. Quite simply, many firms choose acquisitions too quickly, underestimating the effort required to integrate targets well enough to achieve optimal benefits.

But acquisitions rarely provide a quick fix. Sixty-five percent of the telecom executives who chose acquisitions reported encountering friction during integration. The process typically brings unanticipated roadblocks and expenses. And as noted, it is invariably a challenge to retain top talent, who typically have easy access to the best alternative employment options—perhaps with one of your competitors. Chaotic integration could cost you many of those most desirable talents.

Clearly, then, M&A deals are a highly risky resource acquisition strategy. This chapter will help you avoid pitfalls in selecting or rejecting M&A and show how the resource pathways framework can guide your decision.

Can You Integrate the Target Firm?

Despite the many problems acquisitions can create, firms that select them under the right circumstances gain key competitive advantages. As figure 5-1 illustrates, the key question in deciding if the circumstances are right is whether you can feasibly integrate the resources of the target firm.

Integration may occur within the acquired firm, in the acquirer's existing businesses, or in a newly formed business unit and may occur soon after the acquisition or gradually, in stages. In the end, successful integrations create new resources that draw on the skills of the

FIGURE 5-1

Acquisition versus alternatives

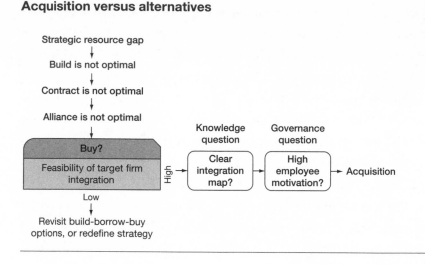

combined firm. Without the creation of new resources, you will almost always overpay for a target. If the target firm merely continues to operate as it did before the acquisition, then your purchase of its shares was little more than a passive investment in the stock market. (See the sidebar "Blended Buy and Build Strategies at Johnson & Johnson.")

BLENDED BUY AND BUILD STRATEGIES AT JOHNSON & JOHNSON

Adding Innovation Strength Through Creative Recombination

Johnson & Johnson is widely regarded as one of the world's most innovative and reliably successful companies. It generates high profits year after year, offering a dynamic mix of consumer products, professional medical products, and pharmaceuticals. J&J's sophisticated sourcing discipline allows it to adapt continuously to changes across its product segments and geographies. This discipline adroitly mixes internal development and acquisitions, combined with active postacquisition integration and realignment.

We tracked the evolution of J&J's medical sector product lines and business units between 1975 and 1997. During this period, J&J operated eighty-eight medical sector business units that introduced eighty-seven unique product lines. Fifty-four of the units originated as acquisitions, and thirty-four were created internally. Of the eighty-seven new product lines, fourteen were innovations developed internally, and the rest grew out of acquisitions. Thus, acquisitions played a key role in J&J's ability to add products—supported significantly by the company's ability to integrate acquisitions into the broader corporation.

J&J is sometimes viewed as a decentralized corporation, one that buys or builds business units and then simply leaves them alone to sell their products and devise their own strategies. But the benefits achieved through M&A went far beyond buying firms and selling their products.

For almost every acquisition, J&J undertakes active integration and realignment, building strong linkages among its units, whether they were acquired or developed internally. In our study, J&J undertook major realignment of about two-thirds of its units within four years of creating or buying them—typically by divesting unsuccessful lines or products that did not fit current strategy and by building bridges between previously discrete units. For example, the company introduced dialysis-related product lines in 1982 by acquiring A&O Surgical and Symedix; it immediately combined the acquired units with a previously acquired cardiovascular accessory manufacturer.

J&J moves to integration as quickly as feasible—though not without giving the company time to learn about the newly acquired unit. Especially with exploratory acquisitions, J&J typically allows targets to operate quasi-independently for a year or more. Still, it fosters learning and information sharing by moving people from its established businesses into the exploratory targets. Upon reaching a critical mass of insight into the technical and market opportunities, the company begins an active business realignment that often leads to the disappearance of the quasi-independent target.

Johnson & Johnson's successful development of the cardiac stent is a striking example of melding resource acquisition, internal development, and realignment. Over more than a decade, from the late 1970s through the early 1990s, J&J bought multiple firms with cardiac-device resources while building internal businesses in the cardiac technical and market space. Over time, as it explored the cardiac area, J&J shifted people among the internal and acquired companies, even as it sold off major parts of its acquisitions.

In 1983, J&J introduced a line of heart valves and other cardiovascular accessories by combining three earlier acquisitions (Extracorporeal Medical Systems, Vascor, and Cardio Systems) into a new operating unit known as Hancock Extracorporeal. In 1984, J&J used Hancock as the foundation of J&J Cardiovascular, expanding its cardiovascular lines and divesting (to Baxter) the dialysis lines that it no longer wanted. Two years later, J&J temporarily exited the cardiovascular business, selling the unit to Medtronic.

In the early 1990s, J&J reentered the cardiovascular market. It developed new cardiac-assist equipment in J&J Interventional Systems, an internally developed unit that it integrated with a specialized cardiac-care acquisition (Menlo Care). The combined business pursued the opportunity to develop early cardiac stents. Then—after more than ten years of development involving a complex mix of people from the different units—J&J combined its emerging stent skills with the balloon catheter lines that the company obtained through its 1996 purchase of Cordis.

The ability to creatively integrate resources across multiple businesses over years of activity led to major market success and billions of dollars in revenues.

To integrate a target firm, you must both *clearly map* the integration pathway and keep the people on both sides of a deal *motivated*. If you cannot identify a clear integration pathway to justify an acquisition, you may be tempted to pull the word *synergy* from your back pocket to use as justification. Synergy occurs when two sets of resources create more value in combination than the sum of their individual values.

However, absent a real understanding of how you will combine resources following the merger, synergy is merely an illusion—one that can dangerously cloud a healthy instinct to walk away from a bad deal.

If you have serious concerns about your ability to integrate the target into your current organization, then you should step back and reconsider. Despite the previously identified shortcomings of other modes, perhaps you should revisit them as options. If they remain infeasible, you should revisit your strategy.

Knowledge Question: Can You Map Integration Clearly?

Integration pathways vary in their clarity. Only occasionally can you define a full integration road map at the outset of a deal. In the simplest cases—such as when you acquire a small firm with a limited set of resources and a short time horizon for using the resources—you can define integration activities while planning the deal. Companies that have active acquisition strategies commonly initiate integration even before a deal closes. For example, GE and Cisco employ well-defined steps for their small- and medium-scale acquisitions.

But many integrations are far from simple; every acquisition target is unique and operates in a unique environment. An integration that works well in your home country may be irrelevant elsewhere in the world. The same is true when the acquisition target competes in a product or market segment not well understood by the acquiring firm. For example, the US-based Bank One financial services company developed strong skills while buying and integrating medium-sized banks in the Midwest. But when it applied those same skills to acquire First USA—a credit-card company—in 1997, the results were much less favorable. The changed context of the First USA deal produced significant turmoil and reportedly led to J.P. Morgan Chase & Co.'s acquisition of Bank One in 2004.

As you analyze the integration questions, you may find it useful to deploy two sets of analysts, a due-diligence practice we've seen in our research. One team is responsible for making the positive case for acquiring the target; the other makes the equally important, negative case. Staff members take turns serving on each team, so that no one becomes typecast as a corporate naysayer. Senior management assesses both cases and makes a final decision. While this approach requires extra analysis, the companies in question have found it invaluable. They not only avoid bad deals, but also gain a better understanding of the deals that they undertake. Moreover, the two-team approach has fostered a powerful, disciplined, cooperative spirit among company staff.

But however you structure the integration analysis, you need to achieve clarity in three areas for every deal: the scope of resource combination, the scope of resource divestiture, and the timeline of your integration process.

Scope of resource combination

In mapping your integration, you must identify which resources in the target will fill your resource gap. In some cases, M&A due diligence can accurately inventory the target's resources. In other cases, you will only be able to gather in-depth information after the deal closes—when you will need to set up cross-company teams to evaluate the resources.

Resource assessment is particularly difficult in cross-border acquisitions, which can involve very different competitive and environmental contexts, perhaps limiting transparency. A foreign acquirer may lack key information about the quality of some of the desired target resources. For example, a few years ago, a Japanese pharmaceutical firm believed it had scored a coup when it purchased a midsized US life-sciences company. The Japanese firm discovered too late that other US firms had passed up the opportunity to bid because they suspected—correctly, as it turned out—that there were flaws in the life-sciences firm's clinical trials. Similarly, the Chinese bank Minsheng bought a substantial stake in the West Coast US banking company UCBH in 2007 without realizing that the American bank's allowances for bad debts were grossly understated; Minsheng ended up writing off the investment.

Even when both the acquirer and the target firm cooperate in due diligence, it is seldom easy to evaluate resources with precision. After all, executives frequently fail to understand which resources create value in their own organizations, let alone in a target firm. Resources often involve a complex dynamic of internal and external activities, so cherry-picking specific elements can be hazardous. If you cannot form such judgments with confidence, you may need to make a smaller initial investment that buys you time to gain stronger relevant knowledge.

Beware of what seem like tempting shortcuts. For example, if you rely on external help to perform due diligence, you should recognize that a third-party provider will focus on the target's *present* value, not the potential value of the blended assets. The real value of the deal depends on two conditions: how well the target's skills will strengthen, extend, and renew your existing resources and how your own resources will amplify those of the target. Therefore, assessing the benefits of recombination requires an equally complete and acute awareness of both your own and the target's resources and how they will be integrated. To that end, your corporate development and operating staff must be deeply involved in the evaluation. Those decisions must be guided by absolute clarity on the goals of the acquisition; without that, you risk spreading your integration efforts too thinly.

Resource-seeking acquisitions come in three flavors. While any one acquisition may encompass several of these goals, typically one objective dominates:

- *Exploitative acquisitions* strengthen your core domain by adding something new to the resource base to enhance your existing activities in established markets. The added resources enable you to pursue new opportunities that arise in those established markets.

- *Extension acquisitions* extend your existing activities into new geographic markets or enable you to develop new products for existing markets.

- *Exploratory acquisitions* enable you to explore new market spaces; the acquired resources can be disruptive technologies, product categories, or business models.

Clarifying which of these three goals you want to emphasize will help define the scope of your resource combination—which resources to integrate and which to leave as autonomous assets, either to retain or to divest. You will be able to define this scope most precisely with exploitative acquisitions, whose integration must often pool existing resources and sell off unwanted parts of the target, along with portions of your existing business that M&A has rendered redundant. Defining the scope of the resource combination for an exploratory acquisition is typically far more difficult. Exploratory acquisitions may involve targets whose skills you do not yet clearly understand and might conceivably destroy if you were to integrate them into your current organization too quickly. When it comes to the integration of extension acquisitions, defining the scope of resource combination can also be particularly challenging. Acquiring firms typically underestimate the differences in market requirements of a related resource domain or the local adjustments needed to operate in a new geographic market. If you are pursuing an extension acquisition, be cautious about disposing too quickly of local resources that might turn crucial.

The series of acquisitions involving Skype provides a striking example of what happens when a buyer does not understand the scope of integration. When the online retailer eBay bought Skype in 2006 for about $3 billion, the retailer lacked clarity about how to integrate Skype's products. Complicating matters, Skype personnel fiercely defended their autonomy within the new parent firm. In 2009, eBay finally spun off Skype—with a write-down of $1.4 billion—after having failed to combine eBay's strong e-commerce functionality with Skype's voice business. Microsoft, battling to control the consumer Internet market, acquired Skype for $8.5 billion in 2011. Identifying what initially appears to be a clear path to integration, Microsoft anticipates that integrating Skype into its devices and software platforms will make Microsoft's products more appealing to Skype's 145 million monthly active users.

Scope of resource divestiture

In addition to the desirable resources that inspired the acquisition, target firms usually have unneeded resources. Thus, while designing your plan for integration, you also need a parallel process for divesting unnecessary resources—including both the target's and your own. As you integrate the businesses, you must sell product and service lines, manufacturing facilities, intellectual property, and other resources that do not contribute to your strategic goals. Otherwise, you risk collecting a jumble of resources that lead to corporate bloat.

At the same time, the value of many acquisitions lies in how they can help change your strategic goals. In planning for and integrating the target, you will inevitably find that some resources that formerly created high value are now unnecessary.

Firms that engage actively in acquisitions but avoid divestitures are like hoarders, eventually finding themselves overwhelmed by clutter. They become uncompetitive across much of their unconnected businesses, which become attractive targets for more efficient competitors. We take up the discipline of divestiture in greater detail in chapter 6.

Integration process timeline

Integration clarity requires that you understand the timeline. Time horizons differ for exploitative and exploratory opportunities. An exploitative acquisition can be integrated relatively quickly, mainly by aggregating relevant resources and selling off the unnecessary ones. With exploratory acquisitions, however, dealing too hastily with resources you do not yet understand well is potentially destructive. Nevertheless, such acquisitions should not function fully independently if you hope to gain their potential value. Instead, exploratory acquisitions benefit from low-intensity initial interactions that become deeper over time.

When Siemens purchased several small US digital telecommunications firms in the 1990s, it kept them largely autonomous for several years. Throughout that time, however, the German company assigned several corporate engineers to work at the acquired facilities. Only after the engineers had developed an understanding of these units and shared their insights with Germany did Siemens undertake a deeper—and more enlightened—integration. Thus, the pace of integration must be guided by the clarity you possess about the targeted resources.

Although you may be unable to identify even the major milestones of a clear integration process, you may still be tempted to go ahead with the deal while hoping that a clear pathway will emerge later. However, the paths that emerge in such cases often lead directly over cliffs. The only way to avoid disaster is to identify the major goals for the acquisition before concluding the deal and then create a detailed integration plan as soon as possible once the deal is closed. Google, for instance, purchased YouTube for $1.65 billion in 2006, with the goal of connecting online search and video streaming. Google allowed YouTube to operate largely independently for about two years, while the acquirer worked with YouTube's people to develop specific opportunities for the integration. After this initial period of independence, Google then actively connected its own core search business to YouTube's video streaming platform.

You will, of course, never have a perfect blueprint for integration. Still, you must be clear about what you are buying and how its value—in combination with yours—will advance your strategic goals. When Hewlett-Packard acquired Compaq in 2002, HP understood that integrating the two companies' product lines would create strategic value, but it did not have a fully developed road map for how the combined company would generate that value. Rather than attempt to create such a road map up front, HP spelled out the acquisition's major objectives: to expand its presence in the PC sector and to create strong integration between the acquired resources and its printer division. HP then assigned full-time leaders with relevant skills to develop an integration plan and lead the integration activities, which would unfold over a span of several years.

Thus, even without full certainty, HP succeeded because it knew what it wanted from integration and assigned effective leaders both at the top of the company and throughout the operating ranks. And yet, even with strong integration leadership and an understanding of the combined firms' long-term goals, the HP-Compaq integration took almost a decade to accomplish. Along the way, it generated substantial controversy throughout the company. Strategic direction shifted, career paths changed, and traditional business lines were divested. Such complex acquisitions, arising in circumstances that do not suit other sourcing modes, require disciplined attention to integration goals and activities. These may well unfold over many years of work, affecting the lives of people throughout both the acquirer and the acquired.

Government Question: Can You Keep Employees Motivated?

Knowing what to integrate is only part of the battle. In addition, you must know how to govern the integration. Governance includes identifying and retaining key people. You also need to assess whether you have the other resources necessary to manage a potential acquisition—in its own right and in the context of whatever other acquisition activities may also be under way.

Identifying key people

It is sometimes simple to identify key individuals at a target company. But if skills are embedded in teams—as they usually are—then it can be difficult to identify key people and how many individuals you will need to retain. When evaluating an acquisition, part of due diligence involves identifying those people. This is particularly important when you know going in that integration will require dismissing some staff from the target.

It is easy to misjudge which people are most important and to confuse high visibility with high value. No preeminent scientist or star equity analyst works alone; a less visible supporting team is usually critical to overall performance. Therefore, star players must be considered in a team context. Deprived of critical team components, stars sometimes falter after integration, so you may sometimes need to keep valuable teams more or less intact.

Similarly, a target firm's working environment, social networks, and other culture can confound cut-and-dry assessments of personnel. Such factors make it difficult to predict, for instance, whether an outstanding scientist from a small target will become less productive—and more frustrated—once he or she has to spend more time complying with reporting systems at the larger, acquiring firm. To discern the many nuanced contributions of individuals and teams, you might require the "local" insights of target firm managers.

Assessing the target's current resources without clearly understanding their actual origins can also be misleading. A senior executive from a life-sciences firm that was purchased by a multinational pharmaceutical company told us that the firm's scientists were given the most attention and the best retention packages. However, the acquirer failed to realize that most of the innovation had resulted from the target's previous partnerships and acquisition deals—with in-house scientists in a mainly supporting role. In the executive's view, the key people were actually the corporate development people and business unit managers who brought external innovation into the firm.

Thus, when evaluating key resources, do it in context. If a target grew organically, then most of its value was created through R&D, marketing, and other functional resources. If its growth was externally driven, then focus on the key deal-makers and the teams who scan and evaluate external sourcing opportunities.

Retaining key people

Targets need to become integrated as quickly as possible. In part, this means aligning the incentives of *all* members of the corporation—whether newly joined or longtime members. Clearly, no manager will work to implement an integration without sufficient incentives.

The personnel of target companies are often deeply resentful of the acquisition. Many will continue to refer to themselves as working for the target company long after the deal is done. This clear red flag suggests that an acquisition will fall far below its integration potential. Indeed, many such employees will immediately begin searching for new opportunities—with the brightest stars enjoying the greatest number of attractive options. You will need to do everything possible to create a welcoming atmosphere that will encourage a sense of affiliation with the newly combined enterprise. This is not a feel-good obligation; it has a strong bearing on the success of integration activities.

Part of your due diligence, then, involves discovering what incentives—money, career advancement, the lure of a new challenge—will entice key people to stay. If you cannot identify appropriate incentives or you believe that they are unaffordable, you may need to step away from an otherwise desirable deal.

If you do not require target employees' immediate affiliation or, indeed, an explicitly combined entity, you may avoid many short-term difficulties and the cost of some incentives. Leaving the target to operate autonomously within its new parent can help retain key personnel. The start-up life-sciences venture Sirtris retained its independent identity within acquirer GlaxoSmithKline (GSK) for several years after the 2008 acquisition. GSK wanted to preserve Sirtris's entrepreneurial culture and retain valuable scientists whose knowledge differed substantially from GSK's existing resource base.

In our discussions with a Polish investment bank considering the acquisition of a private-equity firm, a senior executive stressed the importance of clearly understanding what most strongly motivates key talent at the acquired firm: "The advantage of a full acquisition is that the acquired team would continue to be responsible for the asset pools associated with their track record, even as we build important connections from our traditional investment activities to the new private-equity business. While their need for *strategic* interdependence is rather low—so that we believe we can connect the businesses successfully—their need for *organizational* autonomy is quite high. Thus, the integration plan for any deal should focus on preserving the acquisition target's autonomy, at least in the short term."

Acquisitions also threaten people at the acquiring firm. Unless the acquirer foolishly puts its thumb on the scale (always a destructive idea), the goals of integration—to produce a rational combination of old and new resources—will necessarily disrupt the careers of some of your current staff. That disruption can be positive. After all, the value of an acquisition lies partly in the opportunity to change the way your business operates. The status quo can become stultifying, and your people may, in general, ultimately benefit by leaving behind obsolete practices and careers. Just as you need to identify key target firm employees whose loss you seek to prevent, you must also do likewise in your existing organization. Who might see the acquisition as a reason to leave? Could you live with that, or would you try to encourage them to stay?

To be sure, you can overemphasize retention. As powerful tools for transforming businesses, acquisitions are by nature disruptive. Inevitably, some people will leave—ideally to pursue opportunities that better fit them and their careers. But if you conclude that a particular acquisition would result in a rapid loss of key people and teams on either side of the deal, then you should reconsider the option.

Motivation is an issue in acquiring firms as well as target ones. Among the telecom companies we surveyed, many acquirers knew they needed the targets' cultures and mind-sets, but were also concerned about disrupting their own staff. One executive highlighted the tension between changing culture and disrupting valuable people: "You buy those companies for their culture. So, actually, you don't want to integrate them into *your* culture; you want to migrate your own people into *that* culture. But that means major reorganization . . . If you reorganize your existing company from top to bottom, you have organization troubles for three years at least." The executive concluded that integrating in a series of small bites would maintain motivation among people on both sides of the deal.

In our interviews across many industries, executives have wondered how best to keep incumbent staff motivated while they import new skills from the target. One senior executive from a leading publisher in Europe was concerned that making too many acquisitions to tap new talent might send the message to his own people that "the best talent and the best innovation is found outside." Indeed, executives from several pharmaceutical firms reported that recent acquisitions had sent a strong signal to their internal R&D staff that they were insufficiently productive and innovative—signals that risked demotivating them.

There is no simple answer here. Your business risks failing if it cannot balance internal with external growth. Acquisitions are exciting because they bring new opportunities. At the same time, they threaten the status quo. You must provide incentives to keep your staff fully engaged with legacy activities even as you are exploring new paths. Helping them understand the coherent vision that inspired the acquisition and how their legacy work will be combined with the target's new resources will calm many misgivings.

M&A execution skills

Finally, you must assess whether you have the necessary financial and human resources to integrate the target firm with your current organization. Postmerger integration often requires far more time and energy than you anticipate, draining resources from core activities. As in the case of HP-Compaq, good acquirers assign strong leaders to manage the integration, often investing in training and recruitment to bolster their M&A teams. During the past two decades, Brazil's Banco Itaú has used M&A as a central strategy for building its leadership position throughout Latin America. The bank's M&A activities accelerated during Brazil's 1990s privatization wave (an active element of the country's economic reforms). In ramping up for its M&A-fueled growth, Banco Itaú drew on a talented pool of managers and in-house and external training and cross-unit rotation programs. The result was a robust and effective capability that helped the bank implement its strategy.

Because any acquisition program entails disproportionately rigorous demands of integration, aggressive use of acquisitions will stretch your company both organizationally and financially—potentially leading to lower performance and higher risk. You will need to exert substantial effort to prevent internal fragmentation and financial fragility.

Binge buying—too many acquisitions undertaken too quickly—may leave little time to digest what's been consumed. Cooper Labs, for instance, grew rapidly in the medical sector through a series of acquisitions during the early 1980s. The expansion succeeded as long as Cooper could integrate its growing set of business activities. But the pace of unchecked acquisitions surpassed its integration limits, and Cooper foundered. Similarly, both Lockheed Martin and Raytheon struggled to integrate several closely sequenced major acquisitions in the past few years. And the India drug company Wockhardt used a series of acquisitions to grow quickly in multiple product markets in India, Europe, and North America after its founding in 1999, only to encounter extended financial trouble in the late 2000s, when the company struggled to make sense of its diverse portfolio.

Such struggles can have major consequences in the market. Tyco's January 2002 announced plan to split into several independent companies—despite strong profitability in 2001—signaled that it had reached the limits of its integration capacity. The company's stock price fell substantially. Tyco had hitherto succeeded in persuading the markets that it was creating value through acquisitions; it had built into its price an expectation of continued M&A-based growth. The market now concluded that it had overestimated Tyco's ability to sustain the pace of integration.

Execution skills are not a guarantee of success. Once firms have pulled off a few opportunistic M&A deals and developed initial tools to execute them, the companies typically get what we call *M&A*

momentum: they opt for the M&A option too quickly, figuring that "we know how to do this now." In effect, they fall into an implementation trap. Only after stumbling in subsequent acquisitions do they eventually realize that overemphasizing M&A yields mediocre results.

Implications for Your Resource Sourcing Strategy

Figure 5-2 summarizes the M&A stem of the resource pathways framework and shows four options that depend on your ability to define the integration process clearly and identify and retain key people at both firms.

The cells in the upper left and lower right of the figure represent more straightforward situations than those in the remaining two cells. The latter two situations raise challenges but also provide opportunities if you can address those challenges—sometimes by making *more complex* acquisition deals.

FIGURE 5-2

Feasibility of target firm integration and resource sourcing options

		Governance question: employee motivation?	
		High	Low
Knowledge question: integration map?	Clear	Feasibility of target firm integration: high *Smooth-path acquisitions* Acquisition	Feasibility of target firm integration: partial *Driverless acquisitions* Revisit options *Alternative*: consider complex acquisitions
	Unclear	Feasibility of target firm integration: partial *Light-in-the-fog acquisitions* Revisit options *Alternative*: consider complex acquisitions	Feasibility of target firm integration: low *Cliff-edge acquisitions* Revisit options

Smooth-path acquisitions

When you have a clear integration map and high employee motivation, acquisitions offer a relatively smooth path to your goal. Even in these optimal conditions, the work is assuredly hard, but your efforts will usually be fruitful. Worldwide, thousands of smooth-path acquisitions take place successfully every year, involving small or large deals in industries ranging from banking, pharmaceuticals, and mining to consumer packaged goods.

In 2004, for example, when Manulife Financial Corp. acquired and integrated John Hancock Financial Services, Manulife had clear strategic goals, mapped an integration path that would achieve those goals, and knew which people to retain to make the acquisition successful. Similarly, the network technology standout Cisco has undertaken approximately 150 acquisitions in the past two decades, working hard in each instance to identify goals, integration paths, and retention strategies, and has seen these smooth-path deals contribute greatly to the company's growth (see chapter 7 for more detail).

Cliff-edge acquisitions

These deals feature both low integration clarity and high risk of employee demotivation. As the name suggests, cliff-edge acquisitions will almost certainly fail—and, in so doing, lead you over the competitive cliff. No matter how hard you are willing to work at implementation, these situations should scare you off.

For example, when the Merrill Dow pharmaceutical subsidiary of Dow Chemical purchased Marion Laboratories in 1989, the acquiring firm had only a limited sense of how best to combine the two companies. It also failed to recognize that many of Marion's key staff would leave. Since the acquirer failed to articulate a motivating strategic vision for the acquisition, many of Marion's most valuable players decided to pursue other options. The loss of key sales executives and experienced managers was particularly damaging, and the combined company struggled to leverage its expanded product lines. Marion Merrill Dow foundered and, in 1995, was purchased by the German firm Hoechst.

Driverless acquisitions

Even with a clear integration path, acquisitions can fail if they lack employee motivation. However, a successful outcome is possible if you can recruit effective leadership to replace key departing executives. For instance, in 2010 the network company Ciena struggled to integrate Nortel Networks' Ethernet business—in part because of the unexpected loss of key players at both firms in the wake of the acquisition.

When you are unsure of your ability to retain key people after an acquisition, several forms of *complex acquisitions* might save the deal. One approach is to break M&A into staged steps, beginning with an alliance or a minority stake and progressing to full acquisition only when the threat of such uncertainties as retention has been resolved. The French food-products multinational Danone took a staged approach when it acquired the US organic dairy producer Stonyfield Farm. Danone entered a joint venture with Stonyfield in 2001 as a minority partner to learn about the firm and the organic-market segment and to check the compatibility of the leadership teams. In 2003, once the leadership of the two companies had established trust, Danone faced fewer concerns about motivation and moved to a majority interest in Stonyfield.

Several other complex-acquisition strategies can address concerns about postacquisition motivation:

- Financial inducements, such as stock options, stock payments, and retention packages.

- Nonfinancial conditions, such as expanded career opportunities and preserving the target's operating autonomy, brands, and customary employment conditions.

- Special considerations with respect to the target's culture. When Walt Disney Studios bought the US animation studio Pixar in a

2006 stock deal, Disney executives agreed to an explicit list of guidelines for protecting Pixar's creative culture. Similarly iconic acquisitions such as Stonyfield; Ben & Jerry's (Unilever); Burt's Bees (Clorox); and The Body Shop (L'Oréal) pledged to honor those firms' distinctive social identities.

• An unusually high degree of autonomy and power granted to the target firm within the parent firm's hierarchy.

In parallel with such measures, you might also consider postmerger indemnification terms that protect you if motivation fails. For instance, when buying state-owned banks, Banco Itaú negotiated a series of government guarantees, including indemnification if strikes were to occur at any of the acquired banks.

Nevertheless, complex acquisitions can be risky. In the 1980s, GM attempted to use complex acquisitions in the form of dual-traded stock—when it purchased Hughes (creating GM-H stock) and EDS (creating GM-E stock)—as a means of motivating key people to remain after the acquisitions. Neither the stock market nor GM could make sense of the combinations, and the automaker eventually spun off both Hughes and EDS. The AOL–Time Warner deal in 2000 is a high-profile example of an expensive attempt to mix highly different businesses in a complex acquisition. After years of intracorporate frustration and conflict, the firms divorced in 2009.

Light-in-the-fog acquisitions

Deals with low integration clarity but high motivation can be called light-in-the-fog acquisitions. Because the steps in these deals' integration are poorly defined, you should assess alternatives before reconsidering such cases. Nonetheless, the high motivation means that people will work hard to make these deals work, so light-in-the-fog acquisitions sometimes offer a potential solution when other options are unavailable and you have enough time to clarify its integration plan.

Walmart's expansion in Africa is a good example. In 2011, it purchased a controlling stake in the South African discount retailer Massmart. At the time of the acquisition, Walmart was unsure how it would use Massmart for its stated purpose of expanding through sub-Saharan Africa. Although African markets are growing rapidly, the potential expansion opportunities in the region are highly uncertain. Despite the uncertainty of the integration strategy, the companies created strong incentives for key executives from the highly successful South African firm to remain with the company and help shape the continental expansion strategy. Walmart was particularly motivated. It had rejected the option of a joint venture or another alliance, because of the substantial resource combinations necessary to exploit the opportunity. It turned to acquisition only after multiple unsuccessful attempts to expand independently in emerging markets.

Other light-in-the-fog acquisitions have been less successful. In 1978, Johnson & Johnson purchased the medical imaging firm Technicare—a leader in the new MRI subfield of the imaging market. But J&J had little sense of how to integrate the target, whose product lines and technology were far from J&J's other businesses. J&J nonetheless worked hard to ensure that Technicare's key scientists and executives would remain with the company, and it provided substantial financial resources to continue MRI and other product development activities. However, with little knowledgeable guidance from the parent company, Technicare burned through a lot of cash, struggling to maintain a strong market presence in the face of growing competition from Siemens and GE. In 1986—after investing hundreds of millions of dollars in the venture—J&J sold Technicare to GE at a deep loss.

As with driverless acquisitions, more complex arrangements can also be used to mitigate unclear integration road maps in light-in-the-fog cases. When you are unclear about the value of the target and your ability to integrate it, you may be able to create deals that address uncertainties about a target's postacquisition cash flows. It is increasingly common for acquisitions of high-tech and private start-up companies to build in milestone components. Young companies often generate little information from which to project future prospects. Acquirers may therefore seek downside protection against information asymmetry or the possibility of unanticipated technological and regulatory challenges.

Life-sciences companies, in particular, have often been burned after paying hundreds of millions of dollars for firms with uncertain product pipelines and no clear path to integration. Recently, some buyers have begun to build contingencies into acquisition deals. Such terms defer part of the payment until a drug or another product moves successfully through trials. In 2008, for example, Dow Chemical negotiated acquisition terms with Rohm & Haas that allowed for reconsideration well into the life of the agreement. When the government of Kuwait rejected a specialty chemical joint venture that Dow had expected Rohm & Haas to complete, Dow reopened the deal in 2009 and negotiated substantially different terms—including ongoing investment support from the Rohm & Haas family trust.

Nonetheless, it can be difficult to negotiate such terms. Sometimes, future technological and competitive conditions are too uncertain to guide formulation of meaningful contingencies; other times, a potential target simply refuses to sell when it cannot know with reasonable certainty how much it will receive in the deal.

Assessment Tool and Summary

Table 5-1 outlines questions that will help you decide whether acquiring your resource partner is the best way to obtain the resources you need. If most of your responses are yes, integration of the target is feasible and you should consider an acquisition. However, if most of your responses are no, you should investigate alternatives.

As discussed, never pursue an acquisition that is ill suited to your context simply because other modes are inappropriate. Even if you don't have a feasible acquisition target, you have two significant options:

TABLE 5-1

Feasibility of target firm integration

Knowledge question: integration clarity		No	Yes
Scope of resource combination	Can we clearly assess the target's resources?		
	Can we define which of the target's resources we want to integrate?		
	Can we define the linkages we will need to create between the target's resources and ours?		
Scope of resource divestiture	Can we identify resources that we will divest from both the target and our existing businesses?		
Timeline	Can we identify for the integration process a timeline that will fit our strategic objectives?		
Governance question: employee motivation			
Target people identification	Can we identify the key people at the target whom we need to retain?		
Target people retention	Can we provide sufficient incentives to retain key people at the target?		
Acquirer people identification	Can we identify our own key people whom we need to retain?		
Acquirer people retention	Can we provide sufficient incentives to retain our key people?		
M&A execution skills	Do we currently have sufficient resources and skills to integrate this target?		

Answer each question about the knowledge fit and organizational fit of the targeted resources. If most of your responses are yes, consider an acquisition (*buy* mode). If most of your responses are no, consider other sourcing options.

abandon your search and revise your strategy, or revisit your earlier sourcing choices.

You may a reluctantly decide that this particular strategic opportunity is too difficult to pursue, and therefore abandon your search for these particular resources. This might seem like giving up, but competition is exciting precisely because it presents you with so many opportunities, some more opportune than others. The closing of one strategic opening frees up bandwidth and budget for the next—perhaps one that will ultimately offer higher value with less difficulty. Strategically, it makes sense to focus on opportunities that are manageable and offer distinct advantage over your competitors.

The European retailer Carrefour is a good example of retargeting. Pursuing the goal of entering the US discount retail market, Carrefour considered purchasing Kmart after having rejected other sourcing options. After careful assessment, however, Carrefour could neither make sense of the Kmart acquisition nor identify another viable target. Rather than spend scarce time and money trying to force the opportunity, the company shifted its focus to new opportunities and a new set of targeted resources—deciding instead to pursue expansion in Central Europe through a combination of internal development initiatives and alliances.

Despite these caveats, you must also beware of giving up too easily on a major opportunity. If the strategic opportunity is big enough to merit additional effort, you might consider more complicated versions of modes you previously ruled out. For example, you might return to the build pathway and consider creating an internal exploratory environment that will allow you to experiment with new resources. You might reconsider the borrow pathways of a complex contract or complex alliance. Indeed, you might reexamine the buy pathway of a complex acquisition. Your pathway will depend on the time and resources available to you and the importance of *this* strategic opportunity relative to others.

Acquisitions are valuable when your strategic goals require new resources to which you are free to make major changes. In such cases, if you can define an integration path, retain key people, and command the skills you need to execute a specific deal, you should seriously consider an acquisition. The best acquisitions involve *smooth paths* with *high integration clarity* and *motivation*. Even if you face moderate challenges in defining implementation or retaining people, then a more complex acquisition may serve you—but only if you have especially strong M&A execution skills. If no acquisition path appears to make sense, you may be better off revisiting previously rejected sourcing modes. Otherwise, you should step back, revisit your strategy, and consider other, more viable opportunities.

Realigning Your Resource Portfolio

We have so far focused on the resource pathways framework to help you select the most appropriate way of obtaining new resources. But the framework has broader utility, because resources constantly change. In this chapter, we discuss how you can use the framework to realign your resource portfolio by increasing control over some resources, decreasing control over others, and completely divesting those that no longer add value.

If you obtained resources and then simply displayed them in glass cases, in the business equivalent of a natural history museum, perhaps they would forever remain in a pristine state. But instead, you put them to work creating new value. They become part of the core of the enterprise, used to advance your strategy. Over time, they are altered and recombined with other resources as your competitive environment changes. What is core today may become noncore tomorrow; likewise, what is now on the periphery might eventually migrate into the core. Whether the value of a resource rises or falls—how rapidly and by how much—depends on forces affecting your company, the industry, the global economy, your customers and suppliers, and the households of consumers.

Resources therefore require frequent reevaluation. As your industry and firm evolve, both the resources you need and the levels of control you seek over them will change. At some point, almost all internal resources become obsolete and you will have to decide whether to shift them into more value-creating activities, revitalize them by combining them with new resources, or divest them.

Divesting obsolete resources is especially important and often difficult. When a firm changes strategy, it must realign its business portfolio and the resources that support it. Divesting resources that no longer fit a strategy allows your firm to shift focus onto new resources. One of the major causes of "accidental" conglomeration in a company is the lack of divestiture discipline. Firms that lack such discipline prolong their attachment to legacy businesses and resources that are no longer relevant to current strategy. Therefore, business leaders must recognize when their resources are losing relevance, and take steps to recycle them into more productive use or, when valuable alternatives do not exist, divest them.

Borrowed resources obtained via licenses and alliances also follow cycles. For example, in the embryonic phase of an emerging technological field, an alliance with partners that offer pioneering products is often a sensible way to gain knowledge despite high levels of product, market, and strategic uncertainty. As the field advances toward a more structured and competitive market, you might seek greater control by increasing your commitment with internal projects or acquisitions. In other cases, once-valuable resources that a partner brought to the alliance eventually lose their relevance—either because of changes in your current competitive environment or because you have learned all you can from your partner. At the technology's mature stage, for instance, you might reduce control by ending a partnership or downgrading a relationship into license agreements if you can retain the benefits of the resources through simpler expedients.

Existing relationships have inertia, however, and will continue indefinitely unless you act—such as by upgrading an increasingly important license to greater control, downgrading a decreasingly important alliance to a less strategic status, or ending a relationship altogether. In the Hero Honda joint venture, for example, Hero's contribution to the alliance lost value over time as Honda learned to operate in the Indian market (chapter 4).

Thus, the way you obtain your resources requires continual reevaluation just as much as the utility of the resources themselves need to be reviewed. Taken together, these complicated evaluations amount to a set of portfolio management activities, rather like the Johnson & Johnson process described earlier. This chapter shows you how you can use the resource pathways framework to keep your firm's resource-management activities well tuned and competitive. In the process, you will also discover that you can improve the long-term outcomes of any ill-advised sourcing decisions that predate your adoption of the framework. First, though, let's look at some cognitive blinders that deter managers from undertaking the continuous assessments we recommend.

Blind Spots: Why Are Executives Reluctant to Realign Their Resource Portfolios?

Firms often become stuck in the past; nearly all experienced managers have seen past choices return to haunt them. So the question is not whether such ghostly problems are common, but why they persist. Several factors contribute to the stickiness of the no-longer-sensible status quo: forward-looking bias, overcommitment to past choices, fads, and fragmented decision-making processes.

Forward-Looking Bias

Firms in dynamic, innovative industries, where executives prefer acquiring new assets rather than revisiting old ones, often have a forward-looking bias. Indeed, a key part of being an opportunity-driven strategist is the constant search for new ways of creating value.

Leaders we interviewed in the telecom, media, and medical equipment industries found it much more glamorous to work on growth opportunities and sourcing new deals than on reviewing and divesting resources. For example, the global head of M&A and corporate development at a leading US medical equipment firm told us that it is "painful to tell a high-achieving general manager that you are eliminating eighty million dollars from his business unit. So instead of thinking long term, we focus on short-term tactics. I reckon that we are not disciplined enough to enforce needed divestments."

But firms need reliable analysis to make rational decisions about the assets they already have. You can, of course, outsource this to your financial advisers. But that creates a different problem—the outsiders managing the divestment often ignore the core resources that underlie the assets being divested. These core resources might have residual value that would make their retention—in whole or in part—worthwhile. The resources that constitute a divested piece of the business can be compared to the now-notorious tranches of subprime mortgages. To be sure, many of the bundled mortgages were toxic, but others were solid and valuable. When divesting an asset, you need to be careful not to throw the baby out with the bath water.

Another consequence of a forward-looking bias is that executives tend to follow the "if it ain't broke, don't fix it" rule. As long as the business is working reasonably well, they devote their energy to finding new opportunities. Yet small problems often escalate. A minor misalignment can become a major wobble. When it does, companies must decide quickly whether the problematic part can be repaired or must be replaced before it causes a crash. In other words, can the existing resource be rejuvenated, or must it be divested? Successful opportunity-driven strategists need to be able to realign existing resources or pare away unnecessary resources, or do both, to create a strong base for continued expansion.

Overcommitment to the Past

If managers aren't dominated by the future, they may very well suffer from the reverse problem: being wedded to the past. This is a particular problem for firms in mature industries. Managers in such firms have invested greatly to obtain new resources. They've spent even more time and effort building a business around those resources. Then, when problems emerge, managers often invest *more* effort defending and reinforcing past choices rather than reconsidering and possibly reversing them. Companies must openly challenge any overcommitment to the past.

Sourcing Fads

Industries often undergo strategic crazes—centralization, decentralization, diversification, reengineering. There are also fads in sourcing modes: M&A can reach wild proportions for a time. Then alliances come into vogue, followed by an intense focus on internal development. Rinse and repeat. Some legacy decisions reflect preferences that held sway across an industry but that no longer suit current conditions. Yet the past is often taken for granted: curiously, when sanity and proportion return to the environment, they seldom reach back into the past to fix what was broken. Firms therefore need to assess periodically whether bygone decisions still make sense.

Organizational Fragmentation

Finally, organizations are often less intelligent than the sum of the people they employ. In your own firm, you have probably seen this scenario: every key decision maker knows that there is a problem with an existing resource and that the company needs new resources and a better resource management strategy to at least partly address the problem. Yet no one will take action. Such inertia stems not from a shortage of smart executives, but rather from organizational fragmentation. The business lacks systems designed—and a culture motivated—to collect and analyze evidence of the problem so that decision makers can identify sensible solutions. Fragmentation is particularly egregious because solutions are not a matter of hiring smarter people; they typically require organizational change.

These four blind spots can easily jeopardize your ability to keep your resource portfolio aligned with your strategy. Let's now look at ways to overcome these blind spots. You indeed need to revisit your past build, borrow, or buy choices and adjust them to their evolving context. Without such adjustment, you may end up with a misaligned resource portfolio, hindering your growth ability.

Revisiting Your Past Build, Borrow, or Buy Choices

Revisiting your past choices requires that you understand the roots of challenges that you now face. When resource-development projects encounter challenges, most firms fall into the implementation trap discussed in chapter 1. They try to cut the costs of using the resources, create new value out of those resources, or push the staff to work harder and longer.

Often, however, the root cause of a resource problem lies beyond the reach of those implementation remedies. People are not underperforming; nor are your resources obsolete. The actual problem is often that the type of control you exert over exploiting the resources is no longer appropriate—and may not have been appropriate in the first place. The solution is to change how you control the resources.

For instance, if you made an acquisition when conditions actually favored an alliance (as described in chapter 4), then you are paying the financial and organizational costs of exerting excessive control. Acquisitions typically exact higher setup and integration costs than do other sourcing options. Organizationally, burdening the acquired firm with the bureaucratic hassles of the acquirer's corporate structure can impair its esprit de corps and innovative productivity. Faced with these prospects, you should explore ways of giving the target firm a longer leash, including significantly more autonomy.

Similarly, changing circumstances could compel you to revisit your borrow choices. Although a basic contract might once have made perfect sense, perhaps you now need more engagement than a contract or an alliance could provide. Rather than invest more time and money in managing a decreasingly valuable partnership, you might need full control over the target resources. Your options are either to buy out your partner or build a new internal competence that replaces the external resources and allows for the needed control.

In revisiting your build-borrow-buy choices, you should distinguish between internalized and borrowed resources. Both building and buying strategies are different ways of obtaining *internalized resources*, that is, new resources over which you can exercise substantial internal control. Whether you developed them yourself or acquired them along with a target firm, the resources have been internalized. By contrast, resources obtained through your contractual and alliances partners are only *borrowed*—you remain dependent on partners for current and future exploitation of the resources.

The distinction between internalized and borrowed resources is crucial when you revisit past choices. You require different mechanisms to change your level of control over internalized and borrowed resources. Table 6-1 summarizes the available options for changing how you manage your portfolio of resources. We discuss those options in detail in the sections that follow.

Realigning Your Internalized Resources

Suppose you have reached a point where your level of control over your internal resources is inappropriate and perhaps counterproductive. Sometimes you need more control over the resources, sometimes you need less, and sometimes you even need to divest them. Let's look at these three situations.

More Control of Internalized Resources

If you are not realizing benefits that would become available with greater control over a project, then you need to further integrate the resource into the mainstream of your company. For example, as described in chapter 2, Hewlett-Packard shifted its internal exploratory unit for printers from the periphery to the center of the company's

TABLE 6-1

Options for realigning your resource portfolio

Type of resource	Change needed for resource		
	More control	**Less control**	**Divestiture**
Internalized (obtained via internal development or M&A)	• Move the internal team or internal exploratory environment into your mainstream organization • Integrate the target firm more deeply within your mainstream organization	• Increase the autonomy of the internal team or unit • Increase the autonomy of a previously acquired firm	• Divest unneeded resources or units
Borrowed (obtained via contracts or alliances)	• Shift from contract to internal project, alliance, or acquisition • Shift from alliance to internal project or acquisition	• Reduce scope and commitment with contractual or alliance partners • Shift from alliance to contract	• End contract or alliance

business activities. HP believed that the printer business had become strategically central—both in its own right and because of the leverage that printer sales created for the company's PC business.

When a firm buys a business to enter a new domain, the target often continues operating with greater autonomy than would be ideal if the acquirer is to gain long-term benefits from the acquisition. Still, as noted earlier, acquirers often allow for autonomy in a target firm to retain key people and avoid disrupting the activities that the acquiring firm does not yet understand. If a target remains fully independent for too long, however, then the acquirer fails to gain the new knowledge, and the potential value of integration is diminished. Thus, firms must integrate the target over time, often in a series of gradual steps.

Gradual integration of the target firm means forging links between it and other units of the acquiring firm, setting up cross-unit teams, and rotating personnel between the target and your other units. In the banking industry, many commercial banks were accustomed to keeping acquired investment banks separate to accommodate investment bank personnel. But such permissive arrangements failed to capture many of the desired synergies. As a correction, the banks attempted to integrate investment activities by forming cross-functional teams of commercial lending and investment executives. If the linked activities failed to produce value, some banks simply exited investment banking altogether. Another example of an ongoing integration is eBay's 2002 acquisition of PayPal. eBay initially allowed PayPal to operate as a largely independent payment option for people who won auctions. But eBay has gradually integrated PayPal into its core business, developing multiple linkages between the auction and payment product lines in the process.

Less Control of Internalized Resources

Sometimes, your strategy will call for *less* control over internal resources, a common situation when you lack sufficient knowledge of the technical and market trajectory of your resources. By creating an internal exploratory environment in these cases, you will have the time and flexibility to investigate the unfamiliar characteristics of particular resources or perhaps to identify a partner that has relevant knowledge and that would help you map out a development trajectory.

Failing to properly understand disruptive technological changes can be perilous. Research In Motion (RIM) faced such a situation with its BlackBerry line when Apple introduced the smartphone. The sales and service organizations that supported RIM's BlackBerry were accustomed to dealing with business users and had little or no understanding of the consumer market. RIM, rather than leverage its strong technical base to leapfrog Apple, has found itself constantly running to keep up as Apple and others push the boundaries of the smartphone market.

In contrast, automaker Toyota managed the organizational challenge of the switch to electronic just-in-time (kanban) systems much better. It understood that eventually, these would replace the legacy, card-based kanban that was a key part of its supply-chain management system. Recognizing that benefits would accrue to the early adopters, Toyota acted quickly. It assigned key people from its just-in-time organization to create a stand-alone unit to pioneer electronic kanban without disrupting the incumbent process. Electronic kanban would require Toyota to adopt a substantially different organizational structure. The company would also need to alter its investment time horizons, create substantially different relationships with suppliers, and devise new ways of training production-line employees. The stand-alone group was free to do its work without interference, insulated from the many internal frictions the new technology would provoke.

Reducing control of key resources is also advisable when you adapt your strategy to seek new market opportunities. When Cisco diversified into the consumer market, it granted more autonomy to acquired units such as Linksys. The company also created a team that was charged with protecting the target firm from the traditional enterprise market business.

Finally, sometimes you need to reduce control simply because a resource has lost value as a source of competitive advantage. In such cases, reduced control can shift the burden of investment and management to a third party. This is often the first step toward divestiture (discussed below). In other cases, reducing control can help a firm benefit from accessing the resources, while not demotivating the people working on their development. When firms, for instance, do not offer a proper incentive system or entrepreneurial atmosphere, it is more effective to shift the resources to the periphery of the organization to allow more autonomy—or crafting a partial or full divestiture agreement.

Knowing how and when to change your level of control over a resource can be difficult. When faced with the biotech revolution, for example, many established life-sciences companies sought to buy small firms that would provide a base of new technology to feed into their regulatory and marketing activities. However, many of the acquiring firms underestimated the organizational differences between traditional small-cell drug research and new genome-based research. Stressed and demoralized by this chasm of misunderstanding, many key scientists left the acquired firms, destroying their value.

Not all firms got it wrong, however. Successful acquirers invested in and engaged with target biotech specialty firms, giving them the freedom to explore new ways of developing drugs and then integrating them only after better understanding their organizational needs. In 1990, for instance, Roche took a substantial equity stake in biotech pioneer Genentech and then allowed Genentech to operate largely independently for many years. Roche refrained from integrating the firm until 2009, when it believed it finally understood the organizational requirements well enough to absorb Genentech and the biotech's product lines into Roche's core business without damaging Genentech's development ability. In such cases, integration is a long-term game. Even now, the success of the integration remains an open question, with many former Genentech employees still concerned about their future in the integrated company—and many traditional Roche employees wondering whether the company is showing excessive favoritism to the Genentech side of the deal.

Of course, the control you relinquish today can lead to misaligned governance tomorrow, if competitive conditions change yet again. Indeed, when less controlled projects, units, and relationships succeed in creating new resources, you will want to maximize the benefits of success. Thus, over time, you must strengthen the links between those independent units and your mainstream organization. Only then will you capture the full value of their resources.

Divestiture of Internalized Resources

At the extreme of less control, it often makes sense to divest internalized resources—including full business lines and units—by selling them to another firm or shutting down related business activity. There are five good reasons for taking this step:

1. Once-valuable resources have become obsolete

2. You are stifling the development of potentially valuable resources

3. Your organization possesses redundant resources

4. Following integration, you identify unnecessary resources

5. You want to correct past mistakes

Obsolete resources

Many once-valuable resources no longer suit market conditions. For you, they are obsolete, but you can often find buyers for whom the resources would be a good fit. If you cannot find a buyer, you may be better off discontinuing their use and saving the costs of supporting them.

Stifled resources

Divestiture can sometimes allow an underperforming unit within your business to operate as a more flexible, stand-alone business, or a new corporate parent might provide it with more relevant resources and organizational support, helping it flourish. The automobile industry is rife with examples of divestitures when acquisitions fail to produce as anticipated. Ford sold its Aston Martin unit to a UK-led consortium in 2007, its UK subsidiaries Jaguar and Land Rover to Tata Motors of India in 2008, and Volvo to the Chinese automaker Geely Automobile in 2010.

Divestitures sometimes trigger a major corporate restructuring. In 2005, Cendant Corp. began to sell off some of its businesses in the real estate and travel industries. The diversified firm had simply become too complicated to manage in the face of dynamic technology and growth in its markets. After an initial series of divestitures, the company split into four separate companies in the real estate, travel, hospitality, and vehicle-rental industries. It ultimately dropped the Cendant name, branding what remained of the business with the Avis and Budget logos.

Redundant resources

As businesses grow—whether by internal or external modes—they frequently also accumulate duplicate competencies, each capable of supporting multiple lines of business. Consolidating and either selling or ceasing some activities can produce valuable economies. In its Ben & Jerry's acquisition, Unilever gained operating efficiencies by combining several production facilities across the corporation. Even a smaller business can generate redundant assets. In the early 2000s, Cisco needed to restructure its technological development activities because of duplicate resource-development efforts of the seventy acquisitions made during the previous decade.

Unnecessary resources

Firms that carry out active postacquisition reorganization inevitably are left with unneeded capabilities—the remnants of the targets' or acquirers' original businesses. Divesting these assets frees up attention and budget that might otherwise be drained, allowing you to focus on new opportunities. In a multi-industry study of divestitures, we looked at 250 acquisitions in the United States and Europe and found that divestiture is a key element of comprehensive reorganizations of both acquirers and targets. The study showed that M&A that led to partial divestitures across the acquiring and target firms helped facilitate resource development in the remaining business activities.

Firms with notably successful acquisition strategies are almost as active in divestiture as in acquisition. Between 1981 and 1987, GE acquired more than 300 businesses and carried out more than 200 divestitures, after extensive changes to the 300-plus targets. Likewise, since 1995 Unilever has made about 250 acquisitions—including such brands as Knorr, Amora, Ben & Jerry's, Slim-Fast, and Alberto Culver—while divesting more than 200 divestitures in restructuring its business portfolio.

Past mistakes

You might also divest as a way of correcting for mistakes that occurred when you originally obtained new resources. The resources might not have fit your portfolio in the first place, or you needed greater flexibility to unlock their strategic value—such that a less integrative mode would have been better. Selection mistakes are common when you explore new resource areas that are unlike your current resource base. Once you recognize a selection mistake, you should divest the unit as soon as you can find an appropriate buyer. Cisco divested its Flip video camera division in 2011 after buying it in 2009. From the outset, Flip seemed an odd fit for Cisco, which is known for its enterprise networking services. Fortunately, Cisco had the discipline to take rapid corrective action.

The best divestitures are those that spin off a unit or sell major resources on an ongoing-business basis, so that the resources maintain value through continued operational integrity: the seller gains revenue from the transaction, and those working with the divested unit continue their careers. However, it sometimes makes more sense to shut down businesses that have become sinkholes for time and money that would be better spent on new opportunities. Unfortunately, many such shutdowns involve units that could have been sold as viable ongoing businesses had firms not waited too long to make a difficult decision. An active and ongoing divestiture strategy ultimately creates benefits for many of the stakeholders with connections to the divested resources.

By helping you identify successful paths for growth, the resource pathways framework makes it easier for you to divest resources that no longer contribute to your growth opportunities. Firms that divest without growing will eventually disappear, and those that grow without divesting will be buried in the chaos of mismatched resources. Both cases show why firms must have both an effective growth strategy and an effective divestiture strategy.

Realigning Your Borrowed Resources

It is likewise important to revisit the level of control you apply to borrowed, but not internalized, resources—those that you have obtained through either a basic contract or an alliance. Because competitive challenges may change the amount of control you need over borrowed resources, you should anticipate sometime needing to change the governance of borrowed resources. The strongest agreements clearly specify the parties' rights to alter the relationship according to negotiated milestones.

More Control of Borrowed Resources

Naturally, borrowed resources are harder to control than those you have internalized. You can increase borrowed resources controllability by upgrading from contract to alliance, or from alliance to internalization. The need for added control arises when you want to significantly adapt a borrowed resource—beyond the terms of an existing agreement—or you face concerns about proprietary rights. Or both. Either scenario is characteristic of dynamic markets, where you need the flexibility to adapt products and services as demand changes and the nature of proprietary rights is in flux.

Flexibility can be a problem in alliances, which must be tightly coordinated with the work of internal units. There can also be challenges if an alliance partner sets up a rival unit or seeks to go in an unforeseen direction. As discussed in chapter 4, Eli Lilly acquired its alliance partner ICOS when Eli Lilly began to research new therapies based on a drug that both partners were codeveloping. Eli Lilly concluded that its own flexibility would otherwise have been limited by ICOS's proprietary rights and that new development efforts would have required too much coordination, over too long a time, for the alliance to continue working effectively.

In many cases, you cannot achieve more control without moving to a deeper relationship. To that end, you might replace or complement a contract with one firm by making an alliance with another. As described earlier, Eli Lilly did this with Boehringer Ingelheim at the same time it had a contract with Amylin Pharmaceuticals. Boehringer and Amylin made competing diabetes products. Creating such a hedge makes sense when the existing contractual partner either lacks the skills you need for a new opportunity or may be unwilling to engage in the deeper relationship you require. Rather than be trapped by an old relationship, your strategy is best served by finding a partner with more appropriate resources.

As with internal resources, the ability to ratchet up control in a borrow relationship can make the difference between competitive life and death when disruptive changes occur. During the 1990s and 2000s, auto dealers strongly resisted US automakers' efforts to change sales and service strategies, often enlisting state regulators in these struggles. The inability to control their dealer networks contributed to automakers' inept response to challenges from Toyota, Honda, and Hyundai—which had tight control of their sales and service strategies.

Similarly, when the US health system introduced a new payment scheme in the 1980s, established providers of hospital information systems were forced to redesign their software. One of our research projects found that providers whose competitive advantages derived from having forged partnerships with specialized hardware and software suppliers were suddenly disadvantaged. They struggled to adapt to the new environment because their partnerships were not flexible enough to negotiate the necessary changes. Conversely, information systems developers that had formerly been disadvantaged because of their overreliance on internal development had the control they needed to adapt quickly. As a result, they won more of the new business in the changed market. Additionally, firms that could shift quickly from a borrow to a build strategy also fared well in the new environment.

Less Control of Borrowed Resources

Sometimes, you will want to reduce your engagement with a partner, even though you still derive competitive value from the borrowed resources. Most often your motive is to reduce the complexity of an engaged alliance, perhaps by downgrading it into an arm's-length contract. Toyota commonly reduces the depth of its engagement with component suppliers once their products have become commodities— after other suppliers have equaled once-distinctive performance characteristics. Strategic shifts are another trigger for recalibration. Corning reduced its depth of operating engagement with the Dow Corning silicone joint venture when the alliance's products and market moved away from Corning's evolving optics business.

There will almost certainly be organizational challenges in reducing control: leaders in affected business units will probably seek to maintain their traditional operating activities—and the power that goes along with them. However, the more you can push your organization to reduce unnecessary control, the more time and resources you free up for control to be applied where it will have more impact and value.

Divestiture of Borrowed Resources

Finally, consider divesting borrowed resources that require less control. In practice, this means ending alliances and contractual relationships that are no longer strategic. Some valuable partnerships last for many years, but most have relatively short, well-defined time horizons for developing and marketing goods and services. When a partnership no longer provides value, you should end it.

Sometimes you can accomplish this by selling continuation rights to a partner that values the resources more than you do. In 2011, for instance, Honda announced it would sell its stake in the Hero Honda joint venture to its Indian partner. The activities in India remained highly strategic for Hero but had become relatively peripheral for Honda, which increasingly focused on activities in North America as well as China and other emerging markets. Other times, partners mutually agree to cease activities that neither partner wishes to continue. In 2003, Bayer and Shell Oil ended a thirty-four-year-old Belgian joint venture to produce specialty chemicals; over the decades, the products had become commodities, losing much of their value for both partners.

To end participation in an alliance or a contract is often a highly sensitive act. As with less complete reductions of control, divestiture affects people in your organization who have had a strong, long-standing commitment to the activity and the partner. From the partner's perspective, a discontinued relationship may mean a major disruption of its business and a loss of reputation. Such losses are felt most keenly by partners who are small players in the industry. Hence, it may be advisable to find a quiet way of ending the relationship—for example, by discontinuing your commitment of resources but not publicly announcing the end of joint activities. Many high-profile deals between large and small pharmaceutical firms have ended quietly, attracting little or no initial attention.

As you can see, the pathways to realign your portfolio are diverse. The sidebar "Realigning the Portfolio: Danone's Transformation into a Healthy Food Corporation" shows how one multinational thoroughly reexamined its resource portfolio and, with great energy and determination, has realigned it to pursue its healthy nutrition mission.

Assessment Tool and Summary

Table 6-2 outlines questions that can help guide your decision either to revise your degree of control or to divest resources. If most of your responses are yes, you need to consider how to exert more control

REALIGNING THE PORTFOLIO

Danone's Transformation into a Healthy Food Corporation

In redefining its mission to "bring health through food to the largest number of people," Danone, the French-based food multinational, has substantially restructured its resource portfolio during the 2000s. The company has shifted its emphasis on staple products such as cereals, crackers, and cookies (or *biscuits* in British English) to concentrate on four key lines in the health-food sector: fresh dairy foods, baby nutrition, medical nutrition, and bottled water. Over half of Danone's total revenues now come from fresh dairy products, where the company has become the world leader with a strong collection of innovative yogurt-based products such as Actimel, Activia, Vitalinea, and Danonino. Building upon this platform, the company has also established itself as a global leader in both infant and medical nutrition. Danone is also number two worldwide in bottled waters. To realign its corporate portfolio with the health-oriented mission, Danone took multiple steps to increase its control over resources within the health and nutrition domains, while divesting resources in "indulgence" categories such as biscuits and alcoholic beverages, which had only limited fit with the new orientation.

Increase Control over Health and Nutrition Capabilities

Build: expand internal R&D. Danone has developed and solidified its health and nutrition resources through years of investments in R&D, of which 50 percent is now spent on probiotics for its yogurt lines. In fresh dairy products, Danone has reinforced its capabilities through multiple steps: increasing its R&D budget, strengthening its R&D community of nine hundred professionals, maintaining the largest lactic acid bacteria bank in the world, and collaborating closely with academic researchers. Danone's commitment to probiotics R&D makes it hard for competitors to challenge its blockbuster product, Actimel. Other dairy companies and private-label manufacturers who have introduced probiotic yogurt using off-the-shelf ingredients have captured only minor market shares.

Borrow: increase control over alliance partners. Danone has increased its control over several partners in the health-food segment. For instance, the company now has 20 percent minority stakes in its Japanese probiotics alliance partner Yakult, as well as an investment in the Indian biotech firm Avesthagen. Danone also took over its US alliance partner, Stonyfield Farm, which is a leading producer of organic fresh dairy products and the fourth-largest yogurt maker in the United States.

Buy: acquire and integrate. Danone has complemented its growth strategy with targeted acquisitions, which it has then integrated within its portfolio. It became the leading vendor of packaged water in Asia during the 2000s, for instance, by acquiring control of Yili and Robust in China, as well as Aqua in Indonesia. In 2007, meanwhile, Danone acquired Royal Numico, a high-profile Dutch maker of baby foods and nutritional bars and shakes. The acquisition helped Danone combine its knowledge of probiotic cultures with Numico's expertise on nutrients for those cultures. Numico also offered strong resources in clinical nutrition and clinical testing, with a strong presence in the anti-aging market.

Divest Resources in Other Product Lines

To realign its corporate portfolio with its healthy nutrition mission, Danone has steadily sold off its "nonhealthy" food businesses. In 2003, for instance, it completed the divestiture of its glass-container line, which was part of its traditional core business. The alcoholic beverage business was an obvious candidate for divestiture because it conflicted with the core mission—moreover, the global beer industry faced strong consolidation pressures. Danone sold its beer business, including France's most popular beer, Kronenbourg, to Britain's largest brewer, Scottish & Newcastle, in 2000. The company also divested its high-margin champagne business.

In the past decade, Danone has divested its biscuit and cracker brands, a sector in which it was once the worldwide number two. Despite nutritional innovations in focused areas such as children's biscuits with higher levels of calcium and lower fat content, the majority of the biscuit market remains an indulgence category, with limited opportunities to leverage health and nutrition skills—the biscuit industry also has low entry barriers and weak protection of innovation. Danone first downsized its biscuit units by closing factories in Europe. In 2004, it then sold its Jacob's biscuits business in the United Kingdom and its Irish Biscuits business in Ireland. In 2007, in the most significant divestiture, Danone sold its biscuits and crackers brands to its main rival, Kraft.

Danone has pursued similar divestitures in other categories that would not contribute to the company's identity as a health and nutrition company, including its sauce, pasta, meat, and cheese businesses.

Adjust Control of Resources in Emerging Markets

Finally, Danone has realigned its resource portfolio to pursue its healthy nutrition mission in emerging markets such as Mexico, Indonesia, India, China, Russia, and Brazil, which now represent more than 30 percent of sales. In India, for instance, Danone set up a wholly owned subsidiary, Danone India, to manage its activities in that country. Danone entered India's flourishing baby nutrition and medical nutrition markets by buying the nutrition businesses of the Wockhardt Group, which had been forced to restructure after struggling to integrate an opportunistic series of expansions during the prior decade (see chapter 5). Danone also terminated its joint venture with its Indian partner, Wadia Group, completing the exit from the global biscuits business. The company has actively pursued alliances in other emerging markets, such as dairy products joint ventures with Al Safi in Saudi Arabia and Alquería in Colombia, and has expanded its probiotics alliance with Yakult to include Vietnam.

Overall, Danone's active resource portfolio realignment—namely, increasing control when it needs greater engagement and divesting once-core businesses that no longer fit its revised mission—have underpinned the company's growth and profitability. Corporate sales grew 175 percent from 2001 through 2010. The company's average annual return on sales grew from 6.4 percent during the 2001–2005 period to 14.2 percent from 2006 to 2010. The value of the company's stock, meanwhile, grew 120 percent from 2002 through early 2012.

TABLE 6-2

Need for resource portfolio realignment

Internalized resources (via internal development or M&A)		No	Yes
Strategic value of internal resources	Do the resources developed by our internal/acquired unit remain core to our strategy and provide differentiated advantage?		
Autonomy of internal/acquired unit	Have we granted too much autonomy to the internal/acquired unit in charge of developing the needed resources?		
	Would the internal/acquired unit benefit from more integration with our mainstream organization?		
External resource availability	Do the internal resources (whether we developed them ourselves or acquired them through an acquisition) remain difficult to obtain through external partners?		
Internal resource redundancy	Do the resources developed by our internal/acquired unit overlap with other internal resource-development initiatives?		
Borrowed resources (via contracts and alliances)			
Strategic value of collaboration	Is collaboration with our contractual/alliance partner becoming increasingly strategic for our firm?		
Competitive overlap	Has competitive overlap with our contractual/alliance partner increased over time?		
Resource leakage	Are we concerned about potential resource leakage or a learning race with our contractual/alliance partner?		
Competitor threat	Have our competitors approached or made alliances with our contractual/alliance partners in key resource areas?		
Capability building	Are we failing to learn what we wanted from our contractual/alliance partners or to build sufficient internal capabilities in the area of collaboration?		

Answer each question about the need for changing the control of your resources. If most of your responses are yes, consider exerting more control over your resources. If most of your responses are no, consider exerting less control over your resources.

over your resources. For internalized resources, consider further integration within your firm; with borrowed resources, consider tighter control or even acquisition of your resource partner. If most of your responses are no, consider reducing or totally eliminating control over the resources. For internalized resources, you can create an internal exploratory environment or consider divestiture. For borrowed resources, you can downgrade or exit the relationship with your partner.

This chapter highlights how you can gain competitive advantages by realigning your resource portfolio during industry, resource, and partnership life cycles. When you need more control, you can shift from peripheral units to central units or from alliances and licenses to internalization, or you can build on what you have learned from your prior activities to identify and integrate a target. When you need less control, you can shift from internalization to exploratory or autonomous units, or reduce the scope of your commitment to a partner. When you do not need a resource, divest it.

Reevaluating resources and revisiting earlier choices can be difficult. Your organization needs the analytical strength to understand the roots of current challenges and sufficient humility to avoid overcommitting to past decisions. A thoughtful combination of these skills can help your business thrive.

Developing Your Enterprise Selection Capability

You now have a robust set of guidelines on how to obtain individual resources and manage those resources over time. This final chapter helps you take what you have learned and build a strong selection capability based on the resource pathways framework within your organization. Our goal is twofold: to help your firm make strong individual sourcing decisions *and* create an organization that is capable of developing and maintaining a balanced build-borrow-buy portfolio across your enterprise.

Figure 7-1 outlines the *selection capability cycle*. You begin by defining a strategic road map and your resource gaps, while avoiding the implementation trap (the mistaken notion that past resource failures resulted from inadequate implementation rather than selection error). When firms struggle to assess their existing resources, they cannot determine what they need to fill resource gaps. Many companies derail at this early stage.

The second step in the cycle is to employ the resource pathways framework as described in chapters 2 through 5 to select the most viable option for obtaining needed resources:

- *Building* through internal development makes the most sense
  when you have a relevant base of internal resources, including
  both knowledge and organizational fit.

FIGURE 7-1

The selection capability cycle

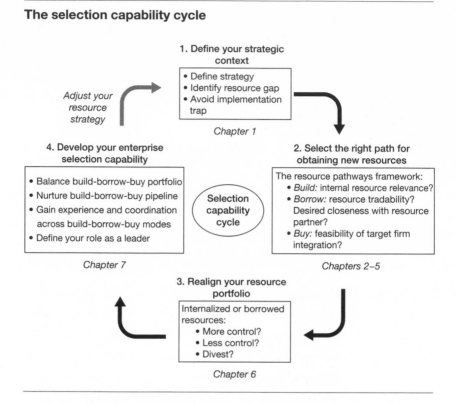

- *Borrowing* via basic contracts provides a superior pathway to new resources when you can both define the resources clearly and protect them with effective contractual terms.

- *Borrowing* by way of a more engaged alliance helps you obtain targeted resources when you and a partner collaborate through limited points of contact and have compatible goals for your joint activities.

- *Buying* resources through an acquisition makes sense when you anticipate needing the freedom and control to make major changes to new resources, but can define a credible integration path and retain key people.

Using these criteria will help you break the grip of bad habits, biases, and vested interests that are the main cause of poor sourcing decisions.

The third step involves using the resource pathways framework to manage your full portfolio of resources over their lifecycles, as described in chapter 6. Since the value of resources is influenced by changes both inside and outside your firm, you must regularly reevaluate the resources' relevance and the way they are used. You might need more or less control of the resources or perhaps need to divest them altogether. You also have the opportunity to monitor, evaluate, and recover from the negative consequences of your firm's past selection errors.

Finally, the last step involves addressing the challenges for decision makers throughout your company—by integrating your resource-seeking activities with corporate development goals:

- Achieve a balanced portfolio of build-borrow-buy initiatives

- Keep your pipeline stocked with internal and external sourcing opportunities

- Accumulate experience using all the modes and coordinating resource-seeking activities across the enterprise

- Define your leadership role in advancing your firm's selection capability

Let's begin with balance.

The Balance Imperative

As we've argued, firms that rely too much on a single mode suffer. Overreliance on acquisitions drains key resources, demotivates and burns out internal teams, and fragments the organization. Too much emphasis on organic growth can make your organization so cohesive that it becomes inert; your internal resources, although unique and distinctive, become a straightjacket that leads only to incremental innovation and limited horizons. Too much reliance on growth via contracts and alliances makes you vulnerable to partners' actions and conflicts of interest.

In contrast, firms that maintain a balanced portfolio of initiatives with different modes of ownership and control can more easily engage with multiple and varied sources of new resources. Over time, they will enjoy many more innovative opportunities than will less multifaceted firms.

Endo Pharmaceuticals is a good example of successful resource mode blending. A specialty pharmaceutical company spun off by DuPont Chemical in the mid-1990s, Endo began its independent life with a small base of internally developed products and a line of externally sourced generic drugs. Over the next few years, the company entered into a series of licenses and focused alliances with US, European, and Asian companies. After building this initial base, Endo began several small-scale acquisitions to complement its licensing activities. The targets provided resources that enabled the company to maintain its internal development skills and thus to create products to sell in the United States and license to European specialty companies. From 1997 to 2011, Endo undertook roughly ten acquisitions and more than forty-five licensing deals while investing about 9 percent of sales in its internal development activities. In the process, the company grew to more than $1.7 billion in annual sales (2010), with ongoing profitability of nearly 20 percent. With its balance of resource sourcing modes, Endo has gained unusual agility in an extremely competitive segment of the life-sciences industry.

Balancing resource modes is important for both established and young businesses. In our telecom study, established firms that used multiple modes to obtain new resources were more likely to survive over a five-year period than those that grew using a single dominant mode. Our study of 3,595 US IPOs between 1988 and 1999 noted numerous delistings among firms that undertook numerous acquisitions during the first several post-IPO years but ignored other avenues to growth. We concluded that newly public firms that become active acquirers are better off pausing after their initial deals, taking time to carefully integrate the targets before pursuing further acquisitions.

For these reasons, before deciding to build, borrow, or buy new resources, you should assess your portfolio of current resource projects. If, for instance, your firm is already stretched because of integration activities related to recent acquisitions, then an additional deal will likely overwhelm your resources and people. If you continue to acquire regardless, your organization will become bloated and unable to create additional growth with the resources you obtain. Transforming your organization into a buying machine will frustrate your employees, who must table their normal development projects to search for new target firms, even as they struggle to integrate acquired firms.

At the other extreme, if you rely exclusively on internal development efforts to generate new resources, then the likely result is an inwardly focused organization that becomes rigid over time. And an overreliance on partnerships will force you to depend on partners' actions, which may reduce your bargaining power and strategic autonomy. Therefore, your decisions for individual resource projects must consider the broader context of your firm's corporate development activities.

Of course, you will seldom have the luxury of managing your firm's resource balance from the very beginning. Typically, you inherit a portfolio of resource projects when you join a company or are promoted. If you inherit an unbalanced resource portfolio, then you will have to adjust it by revisiting past choices while setting new directions for future sourcing decisions.

The timing of portfolio adjustment can vary. Ideally, you will make ongoing, limited adjustments in your resource portfolios. However, firms often need to make drastic adjustments—such as when they have been overusing a particular sourcing mode and therefore need to significantly reconfigure their resource portfolios.

Investors will often urge a firm to make major adjustments if they believe it is being damaged by portfolio imbalance. For example, the

CISCO'S CORPORATE DEVELOPMENT PORTFOLIO

A Dexterous Blend of Sourcing Modes

Cisco, the world's largest maker of networking equipment, has grown from two employees in 1984 to more than seventy thousand people, two hundred worldwide offices, and revenues of $43 billion in 2011. Besides its well-earned reputation as a best-in-class acquirer of innovative high-tech companies, Cisco is also adept at complementing acquisitions with strong internal development and alliances. Its balanced approach is rounded out by corporate support activities—in-house venture expertise, strategic use of flexible incentives, an expansive resource-scanning horizon, and robust execution skills—that keep it well supplied with new resources and customer-oriented solutions.

The base strength of Cisco's corporate development is its ability to carefully evaluate sourcing options and engage adaptively and creatively with internal and external innovators. In the way it blends all the modes, Cisco demonstrates the value of top-level leadership for what should be seen as an enterprise discipline: strategically coordinated building, borrowing, and buying.

Buying: Cisco is best known for its successful acquisition strategy, beginning in the 1990s, when it bought and efficiently integrated about seventy entrepreneurial firms. The young company quickly obtained the complementary technologies needed for leadership in the fast-growing market of routers and switches. In the process, Cisco honed a thorough and efficient due-diligence process. Its selection criteria emphasized small, fast-growing companies that were highly focused, entrepreneurial, and close to Cisco both geographically and culturally.

Entering the new millennium, the company sought growth outside its core base of business customers. It made challenging platform acquisitions in the consumer market: Linksys, a maker of home networking products (2003), and Scientific Atlanta, a developer of cable TV set-top boxes and other home broadband equipment (2006). In doing so, Cisco needed to adapt its acquisition processes. In particular, because the new resources were a departure from Cisco's traditional customer and product segments, Cisco built in more time to explore the new markets before fully integrating the acquired firms.

Building: Cisco's mainstream internal-development teams work to continuously improve and make breakthroughs in the company's core technologies (routers, switches, and other networking products). Historically, Cisco has devoted more than 10 percent of sales to R&D (including an average of 14 percent from 2009 through 2011).

Building via intrapreneurial activities: To complement mainstream R&D, Cisco supports the development of small, autonomous teams. Such intrapreneurial ventures have led to the creation of several spin-off companies. Occasionally, Cisco has reacquired spin-offs as spin-ins (explained later in this chapter). Supporting intrapreneurial behavior helps Cisco incent promising innovators to stay connected to the company and gives the company a privileged window onto the knowledge being developed by its most entrepreneurial employees.

Borrowing via alliances: Cisco applies a similar corporate discipline to engaging and managing alliance partners. Each alliance is managed in the context of its own life cycle, with unique performance metrics and anticipated milestones for progress and goals spelled out. The company monitors changes in any collaborative relationship and will adjust its commitment accordingly. This active reevaluation allows Cisco to respond quickly to new information—adding or subtracting control as alliance value rises or falls.

Borrowing via basic contracts: Cisco uses contracts for development and production activities. Most of its manufacturing is done by contracted providers. The company has developed a template of terms for such deals, including quality, cost, and delivery requirements—including manufacturing logistics specifications for continuity of supply, inventory management, and capacity flexibility.

Borrowing via corporate venture activities: Cisco has an active venture-capital arm whose mission is to scan and engage with external partners across the world in new strategic and geographic areas. In its external scanning, the company assesses not only the targeted partner but also the vitality of the partner's ecosystem—for example, the surrounding universities and labs, the riskiness of the political and economic environment, and the degree of development of the local venture-capital industry. When engaging with a firm in a distant and unfamiliar market, Cisco often partners or invests with a local venture fund. Absent such uncertainty, it invests directly in the firm by taking a minority stake. If a partner proves to offer high strategic value, Cisco will eventually increase its stake to gain full control.

Borrowing via crowd-sourcing: Leaving no stone unturned, Cisco has run several open global competitions in which outsiders are invited to propose ideas for new Cisco products. The ideas are judged (by a panel of Cisco technologists) on their fit with Cisco's strategy, the quality of their innovation, and their potential to become a billion-dollar or greater business. Winners receive a six-figure prize and the chance to participate in developing the idea—in which Cisco will invest up to $10 million over a three-year period. Such innovation tournaments are a genuine outlier mode for obtaining ideas from potentially knowledgeable crowds—Cisco's entrant pool includes many talented engineering-school grads and students. Evaluating a thousand or more complex submissions is the labor-intensive downside—though well worth the effort if an idea really pans out.

Chicago-based media giant Tribune Company faced significant shareholder pressure in 2006, when its stock price fell to half its 2004 value. It divested $500 million in noncore assets, a move accompanied by a stock buy-back program. Similarly, a company whose internal R&D pipeline is depleted may be pressured, either by investors or by its board, to be more aggressive in seeking external resources. But be careful not to veer from one favored extreme to the next. The sidebar "Cisco's Corporate Development Portfolio" highlights how Cisco uses both internal and external sourcing modes to develop its resources.

Many companies—or new CEOs hired to correct past mistakes—fall into the trap of following a simple cycle in which they concentrate first on one resource sourcing mode and then on another. After first emphasizing organic growth, perhaps, they embark on a cycle of acquisitions to overcome the inertia of excessive inward focus, later to pursue new organic growth to correct the overreliance on acquisitions. Though it can be difficult to avoid cyclical sourcing preferences, you have the tools to manage them in a way that achieves balance, overcomes the whiplash of careening, and steers clear of competitive shoals.

Even GE, one of the world's most admired companies and a highly profitable global player in multiple industries, fell into this cycle trap. During the 1980s and early 1990s, the company used a nuanced combination of internal development, contracts, alliances, and acquisitions to drive its global growth. Yet, as it achieved global scale and scope—with revenues over $100 billion by the late 1990s—GE began to favor acquisitions to drive continued growth. It substantially decreased internal investment and external partnerships. Both R&D, as a percentage of sales, and the number of new alliances declined strikingly.

As a result, GE began to suffer competitively: internal skills began atrophying, and the firm found it increasingly difficult to integrate acquisitions. One of the early strategic changes that Jeffrey Immelt made when he took over as CEO in 2001 was to renew the company's commitment to internal investments and alliance activity. Although GE continues to purchase dozens of targets each year, its balance is much improved, with higher rates of internal R&D and strong alliances throughout the world in key areas such as energy, aerospace, and health.

The challenge of maintaining balance is felt across all industries. In 2011, Unilever announced a recommitment to organic growth in the consumer goods industry. The company leveraged its brands in emerging markets to complement growth the company had previously achieved through acquisitions and regional alliances.

In pharmaceuticals, Sanofi-Aventis found itself with shortages in its drug pipeline during the mid-2000s because neither its prior internal development efforts nor the drugs it had acquired through M&A were paying off. A series of acquisitions produced only limited success in obtaining new products at reasonable prices; worse, the firm struggled to integrate targets' resources. New leadership has recently taken a more balanced approach to selecting sources of opportunity. While continuing to invest in internal development and selective acquisitions, Sanofi-Aventis became much more active in pursuing licenses and alliances. Market reaction was positive, with the company's share price growing steadily and outperforming the pharmaceutical industry as a whole following the changes.

There are obvious risks associated with riding sourcing cycles. Firms that become fragmented from making too many acquisitions, for example, might radically compensate by overintegrating targets. Or a firm that has grown frustrated with the progress of internal development efforts might rush to complete alliances and acquisitions—at the risk of undervaluing its own employees while allowing the degradation of a strong internal knowledge base and skills.

Nurturing Your Pipeline

There are two important ways to stock the pipeline with sourcing choices: first, you must regularly scan internal and external domains, engaging with innovators in both environments. (Surprisingly, many executives are ill informed about activities in their own firms' R&D enclaves.) Second, learn to use tools that will help you cultivate external exploratory options. Cisco exemplifies a firm that actively replenishes its pipeline of sourcing options (see the sidebar "Cisco's Corporate Development Portfolio").

Internal scanning might seem to be an easier task than external scanning—the universe is certainly more circumscribed. However, many executives we interviewed emphasized the many obstacles (especially in larger companies) in locating and using knowledge within their own walls. Internal people commonly lacked familiarity with resources and knowledge of their own sister units. Obstacles to knowledge sharing are especially entrenched in companies with hierarchical cultures and strong functional organizations, or in companies characterized by fierce internal competition between business units, teams, and individuals. In such cultures, employees will be reluctant to use a best practice from a sister unit if doing so threatens their own status in the firm. In the absence of viable internal information channels, it is easier to find and exploit external knowledge than internal knowledge.

Firms that recognize the challenges of identifying and connecting internal resources often invest in corporate knowledge centers, best-practice databases, skill inventories, and knowledge maps. They also develop incentives for employees to free up time to identify and share knowledge. A European IT firm we studied used a "knowledge capture and access" project to generate company-wide discussion, open to all employees, over the corporate intranet. The firm complemented this project with a "knowledge trading" service that diffused experience and knowledge across units and layers within the firm.

Companies often find it difficult to retain key personnel and to control proprietary ideas. Star employees are often mobile; they may join other firms or create spin-offs (increasingly, in both developed and emerging markets). For this reason, companies must work hard to remain engaged with key employees. Some firms attempt to protect the value of internal resources by using defensive mechanisms, such as noncompete restrictions. But such measures can cut both ways, often making it hard to attract the best talent in the first place. On the other hand, creative incentive systems can help maintain internal engagement by giving innovators a financial payoff while allowing the firm to control successful resource-development projects.

External scanning is much more challenging. The sheer volume of accessible resources is exploding as innovations in every industry emerge from all corners of the world:

- The growing global availability of private venture-capital finance creates ever more widely distributed start-ups. It would be costly to identify and monitor even a subset, let alone all relevant sourcing options.

- Private firms and emerging-market firms are often invisible to scanning.

- Even firms that would like to be found may lack the financial resources, networks, or mind-set to use financial advisers who might bring them to the attention of resource seekers.

Together, these factors stifle the formation of truly wide-net resource markets. Resource-seeking firms often miss opportunities, and private sellers typically end up with a narrower pool of potential bidders. In one of our studies, only 8 percent of private targets were bought by an acquirer outside their industry, compared with 24 percent of public targets.

Although external scanning can be costly, if done sensibly it will allow you to identify license, alliance, and acquisition opportunities within your ecosystem. Depending on the nature of your company, resource scanning can take many forms. Big corporations often have a dedicated corporate development team—and sometimes a corporate venture practice—and a corporate chief technology officer and technical staff. These units all follow market trends, assess emerging resources, and identify external innovators (often causing substantial duplication of effort while operating with little coordination). After screening external resources, the corporate development team works on the deal. The chief strategy officer (or similar leader) of such a development team needs to combine internal and external views to create a diverse picture of strategic resource options and potential sourcing modes.

Though smaller firms may have little formal scanning structure, the work is no less important. Often, it is done by one leader or—to better effect—a group of senior executives (perhaps a chief strategist, a chief technology or an innovation officer, and a business development leader). Leadership would be responsible for scanning external resources, negotiating with resource providers, and assembling and evaluating internal and external resource opportunities. External consultants and financial advisers can also help identify resource, partnership, and acquisition opportunities.

Partial Acquisitions

If the full acquisition or full control of a target firm is not optimal, an equity stake will help you access the firm's resources and monitor its activities. Even relatively small "educational investments" are especially useful at early stages of resource creation. You get to learn from the target firm without a full commitment or disrupting the target firm's work and possibly leading it astray. This level of investment is a sort of prelude to a more significant equity stake. Depending on its size, an educational investment can lead to greater sequential stakes that give you considerable control of the target firm. Many resource-seeking firms want to reach an equity threshold that provides preferential access to the target—achieved by gaining a seat on the partner's board and enjoying decision making and voting rights. Corporate venture practices at Intel, Cisco, and other established high-tech firms play important roles in guiding early-stage companies' development.

Equity stakes can serve several purposes. They may be stand-alone investments that provide preferential access to a target firm—typical for highly uncertain, exploratory projects. They can be used as hostage instruments to help align your interests with those of your partner. They can reinforce the operational and financial linkages that two firms form through licensing or alliance agreements. Such alignment is especially important when you and your partner will be mutually dependent during a long development cycle. Indeed, equity stakes are common for licenses and partnerships between biotech and large pharmaceutical firms. Genzyme, for example, entered into a $325 million licensing deal with Isis Pharmaceuticals to commercialize Isis's lipid-lowering treatment for high-risk cardiovascular patients; Genzyme also created an alliance to colead the clinical trial. As part of the deal, Genzyme purchased $150 million of Isis's common stock.

Spin-Ins

A *spin-in* is a transaction whereby a resource-seeking firm and an external innovator agree on a set of milestones that would trigger an acquisition if the innovator achieves the specified goals. Such agreements fund innovators' development activities and give them the flexibility to work independently. In 2001, Cisco invested $84 million in a new fiber-optic switch company called Andiamo. Three years later, Cisco paid a reported $750 million to exercise its right to acquire Andiamo. The spin-in agreement specified a purchase price range (up to $2.5 billion) based on a formula that factored in Andiamo's sales levels.

Some novel spin-in transactions take the form of a "spin-out to spin-in" sequence. Suppose an employee develops an idea for a new business and leaves the firm to pursue the project. This is likeliest to happen with ideas at the bleeding edge of a new technology category in which the employer is not yet ready to invest. If the former employee's new venture shows initial success, the employer might spin it back in and work closely with the employee to move the business forward. Some firms have made a discipline of this model: DuPont Chemical long followed a policy of encouraging employees to set up their own businesses—using DuPont as a supplier—if they developed innovations that DuPont did not want to commercialize immediately. (For instance, W. L. Gore & Associates, known best for its waterproof fabrics, built its diverse product lines around DuPont's PTFE polymer— which one of the company's founders had researched as a DuPont chemist.) And many of Cisco's recent spin-in deals have involved companies that either employ or were founded by former Cisco executives. (Cisco and other high-tech firms actively encourage "alumni associations" that maintain connections between the companies and their former employers. This creates an extended community of potential innovators in which to scan for new resources.)

Note that spin-in negotiations present substantial challenges to both buyers and sellers. The buyer needs to incentive the innovator to create resources the buyer will value. And the seller must tailor its resource-development activities to the needs of a particular buyer— which may limit the seller's future bargaining power. This means that spin-in transactions most commonly involve innovators—including former employees and consultants—who have experience with the resource-seeking firm.

Investing in Venture-Capital Funds

At an early stage of technology development or in unfamiliar markets, investments in relevant venture-capital funds can help you identify and benefit from disruptive advances in new resource areas. In the process, you also spread out the risk and management responsibility. In 2008,

Cisco invested in the regional venture fund Almaz Capital Partners to explore the potential of technology start-ups in Russia. Almaz Capital Partners focuses on small and medium-sized technology, media, and telecommunications companies that promise high growth; it scans for such investment opportunities and manages the fund's portfolio.

Whether their focus is geographic or specialized technology segments, venture funds can be a good way to gain deeper knowledge about local ecosystems, targeted resources, and viable partners. It is a nearly pure learning opportunity, since selection and management of the early-stage companies is up to the fund itself. In due course, if investments show promise, you can progress to direct equity stakes or more substantial licensing, alliance, or acquisition deals.

Engaging with external innovators is challenging if you lack credibility as a relevant player within the targeted resource domain or when the innovator simply does not want to sell its resources. The innovator may propose some form of collaboration as an alternative. But if you cannot find a way to engage satisfactorily with a third party, consider whether an internal exploratory environment could meet your needs.

Gaining Experience

As with any activity, you do better with experience. It is far better to seek experience proactively than to sit back and wait for an urgent, competitive imperative to push you, unprepared, into a scarily unfamiliar task. As part of their ongoing growth strategies, businesses must actively seek opportunities to flex their muscles—participating in resource-seeking activities that range from internal projects and exploratory environments, to contracts and alliances, to major acquisitions.

Typically, your firm's size will shape how you gain experience. Smaller firms will more often rely on internal development, contracts, and alliances and will find it difficult to acquire other firms. Nevertheless, even a small firm can sometimes seize a high-growth opportunity and pursue a focused acquisition. Moreover, our research shows that firms that actively learn to use contracts and alliances to complement their internal development activities will grow faster than those that rely only on internal development. They also more quickly reach the level of competence and confidence where targeted acquisitions become viable.

A firm's history and ingrained sourcing practices also matter. Most firms begin with internal development and move later to external sourcing options. Their challenge is to move beyond their historical walls before becoming trapped. Some businesses, though, begin life by using licensing or alliance partnerships and might even quickly form networks of partnerships. In such cases, the challenge lies in building sufficient internal strength to complement the resources obtained through partnerships.

Proactively building up your firm's sourcing experience will quite likely require overcoming the resistance of entrenched groups and leaders. As we've seen, resistance has its roots in the blind spots we've discussed in previous chapters: powerful M&A teams are often reluctant to turn a prospective acquisition deal into an alliance. Your licensing team might not see the value of a full acquisition. Internal staff may have a hard time accepting the distinctive quality of third-party resources. The assorted biases of the CEO and other members of top management further complicate historical preferences and can also strongly influence the paths that your company selects. Some leaders are compulsive shoppers and use their deal-making savvy to expand their companies; others have the souls of inventors and engineers, leading them to prefer internal development and the integrity of organic growth.

Achieving Coordination

Most companies of any size have multiple staff and line groups with formal or informal responsibility for deciding on internal development projects, leading acquisition activity, and managing contractual and alliance partnerships. Unfortunately, these groups often operate with limited intergroup coordination. Management of internal development might be located deep within operating units, M&A leadership may function as a corporate development group, and partnership strategy decision making may be scattered through multiple operating units.

Although myriad combinations of structures and systems exist, the unifying theme is this: no designated authority pays all-encompassing attention to the quality of enterprise sourcing decisions and activities. Perhaps it would be more apt to call this a "dis-unifying theme," since in most organizations, no one sees the full picture.

Coordinating sourcing decisions at the enterprise level is rare. An executive from one global company recently spoke to us about substantial leadership fragmentation over the use of resource modes in his company. Although the CEO paid close attention to acquisitions, he was uninvolved in decisions about alliances and licenses. In our experience, even firms that actively use all the modes for obtaining resources often struggle to recognize which to use in particular cases. This results in major missed opportunities to obtain strategic resources. If powerful resources are obtained through the wrong sourcing mode, the outcome typically brings difficulty and disappointment. Such uncoordinated activity is the death knell of any attempt to establish a reliable means of properly selecting and balancing your resource portfolio.

To overcome ingrained habits and conflicts of interests, your build-borrow-buy decisions require strong oversight. A chief strategy officer or another senior leader can provide guidance and help adjudicate trade-offs among different aspects of corporate development activities. Yet because a single executive can seldom coordinate all major sourcing decisions across a firm, you will need to develop a more extensive selection capability that engages multiple decision makers. There are two main ways of accomplishing this: a strongly integrated approach and a distributed approach.

Some firms have created an integrated corporate development group with responsibility for the full scope of build-borrow-buy analysis and implementation. At a leading IT firm we've worked with, the person responsible for corporate development has fostered collaboration among members of the strategy, M&A, and venture-capital staffs.

"In many companies you would see a split between these groups," he told us. "We keep them all contained within my team. Every individual participates at all the various points along that life cycle."

In reality, however, most firms maintain discrete groups for each sourcing activity. Indeed, each mode requires enough time and attention—and a specialized set of execution skills—that it often makes sense for different people and groups, at different operating and staff levels, to take lead responsibility for internal development, partnership, and M&A strategy. In such cases of specialization, each group should agree on a robust set of selection rules and then actively communicate with the other groups, ideally engaging with them during selection analysis. This makes it easier, for example, to shift responsibility for exploiting a particular opportunity from one business unit to another so that your business can act quickly, lest the opportunity disappears.

The South African telecom firm MTN illustrates the power of distributed responsibility for identifying resource paths. MTN expanded across Africa through a careful series of acquisitions. The company realized that its South African knowledge base could help it coordinate a pan-African cellular network, but it could not by itself provide the primary knowledge needed for such an extensive expansion. MTN therefore undertook the following measures:

- It built strong relationships with governments and regulatory bodies throughout the continent. When a privatization wave swept through many African countries, the firm leveraged its government relationships to purchase many local telecommunications companies.

- MTN concentrated on creating a common brand and set of coordinated operating systems across the continent.

- It developed strong local organizations in each country.

- The firm used its aggregate mass presence to introduce innovative services (such as the mobile phone-banking service developed in partnership with Standard Bank).

The combination of targeted acquisitions, expanded operating systems and brand (through leveraging a strong knowledge base), focused alliances, and targeted local development has been hugely successful. In identifying appropriate growth paths, leadership began at the top of MTN, with the chairman and the CEO, then percolated down to executives who took the lead in specifying the appropriate mix of growth modes for each country. It was strategically wise of MTN to resist imposing a single, inflexible corporate-wide approach to growth for all countries in Africa.

To succeed at choosing among different sourcing paths, coordinating multiple enterprise-wide new resources, and handling these activities' resultant organizational tensions, you have to experiment and learn. In the process, you will be helping managers create and refine a vision, prioritize strategic goals, and test the goals against available resources and the pathways for obtaining them. As you and other decision makers gain experience using the selection criteria, it will become easier for your firm to maintain a balanced resource portfolio.

As pointed out in chapter 1, no amount of implementation ability can compensate for a poorly chosen resource pathway. Still, you need to factor in implementation skills when choosing which path to follow. If implementation without proper selection makes you miss the right path—no matter how hard you work—then selection without strong implementation skills makes you fall off the right path.

Developing a strong selection capability will bring your company major competitive advantages. Now, it is up to you to plant the seeds of this capability. It won't happen overnight. Just as farmers prepare their fields, you must prepare your organization.

Your Role as a Leader

You have probably experienced the frustration of returning from an exciting, idea-packed conference only to find that the people back at work are unable to share in your excitement. After all, while you've been away, they've had their heads buried in the day-to-day grind. Try as you might to explain what you learned, they're not getting it at all. The resource pathways framework will face this fate unless you can help decision makers recognize its potential enough to give it a try. That first step is decisive. Your mission as a leader is to cultivate, step by step, your firm's ability to use the framework as an essential component of corporate development.

Creating Shared Understanding: Discussion, Action, and Diffusion

Your first leadership goal is to create a shared understanding of the power of the resource pathways framework. That requires three basic steps: discussion, action, and diffusion.

First, *discuss* the framework with decision makers in your business. Your focus should be pragmatic. You want to persuade a few strategic leaders—people with sufficient clout, courage, and creative imagination—to authorize a proof-of-concept experiment or two. Ideally, therefore, these leaders should already recognize that the firm's problem with growth is related to a chronic shortage or underperformance of strategic resources. Discussion must be framed as a call to action.

In chapter 6, we described a major pharmaceutical firm that struggled to fill its pipeline with internally developed drugs, a challenge that threatened the company's competitive position. To address the problem, a senior executive convened an informal working group of people from the top management team and the development labs. The executive began by spelling out the problem: a default preference for internal development had choked off valuable external ideas and led to stagnation. Key competitors had leapfrogged the firm by mixing internal development with licenses, alliances, and acquisitions. The working group members—including laboratory leadership—agreed that the company needed to become more open to outside ideas and assets. The company began a series of licensing deals, alliances, and small-scale acquisitions. Within three years, it had succeeded in replenishing its pipeline with promising drugs in various stages of clinical development.

When discussion occurs in the context of a known problem, it typically moves quickly to *action*. Use the resource pathways framework to achieve early wins. Success will build commitment. Identify opportunities that will visibly contribute to the firm's strategic goals. People—especially those accustomed to simply diving in—often grow impatient with the demands of a new process. Therefore, you must credit the step-by-step guidance provided by the framework for making the difference between success and yet another disappointment.

Don't tackle Kilimanjaro too soon. Your early wins will often be small-scale ventures that you can carry through quickly with a small core group. Sometime, you will be lucky enough to identify early opportunities for the framework to deliver disproportionate impact. The key is to pick projects that have a high chance of success. When Steve Jobs returned to the CEO position at then-struggling Apple Computer in 1997, he rejected a long, drawn-out analysis. Instead, he simplified the company's product lines and then quickly moved from a default internal strategy for technology to one with a few key external opportunities.

Diffusion won't happen virally; it needs help. To diffuse the framework throughout your organization, you need to fan the flames of your early wins. Leverage the people who participated in those successful projects to help build a network of colleagues who see the potential and are eager to find opportunities to use the framework themselves. Well-placed expeditionary networks can build momentum quickly, even within a large organization—and especially if the grapevine fills with talk of the early wins. At Apple, the initial success of the improved Mac platform drove the iMac's increasing market share that, in turn, led to branding and development advances. These solid steps toward recovery ultimately contributed to Apple's later success with the iPod and other products.

You need to generate a cascading effect once leaders throughout your organization begin to see the resource pathways framework as indispensable to their own specialized activities—identifying internal development projects, leading an acquisition strategy, or designating a particular functional group to take the lead on a project. Beyond their own purposes, specialists also need to understand that a strong selection capability requires an organization-wide outlook that seeks the best solution for the *enterprise*—not for a particular function, activity, or leader. For example, you want your firm's acquisitions team to bow out once the team recognizes that a particular opportunity is better suited to be led by a team with internal development or partnership responsibilities.

But how formally should you embed the selection capability within your organization as the skill diffuses? It makes sense to begin informally, perhaps using a Skunk Works, such as we described in chapter 2. Over time, as you gain experience and achieve success, increase the formality of activities. Eventually, establish selection analysis as part of your strategic planning cycles—ideally with you or your group of early adopters taking substantial responsibility within the planning process.

The transition to a formalized use of the framework depends on the speed with which you can diffuse it. Several factors affect speed: organization size, structure, and geographic dispersion. Naturally, smaller organizations diffuse new skills more quickly than large ones, often through informal means. Geographically dispersed firms typically take longer to diffuse skills and need more formality—which is useful in engaging people in far-flung regions. New skills tend to diffuse faster and remain informal in relatively flat organizations, whereas hierarchical companies have slow diffusion and greater formality. Identifying such contingencies will help you determine the diffusion path and degree of formality that make sense in your situation.

Also consider how executive turnover might affect your ability to use the resource pathways framework. Invariably, leaders in dynamic organizations—and even entire leadership teams—move regularly, sometimes to other firms and sometimes to different parts of the company. Such churn can disrupt systems and processes, including diffusion of the framework. Of course, if you are the person who is moving on, you can carry the framework to a new organization. But if instead you lose colleagues who were important allies, you face the challenge of finding and engaging new support. You must act quickly. Lost links in a network of advocacy can damage the cause of diffusion. Underscore the role that the framework has played in generating new success in the business.

Leadership at Multiple Points in a Firm

Your leadership role in developing a strong selection capability in your firm will require different approaches, depending on your position. If you are a senior manager, you are well positioned to make adoption of the framework a priority within the strategic planning and implementation skills of your company. If you work in a midlevel staff position or in an operating unit, begin by building a local selection capability to help guide the strategic activities for which you are responsible, only later seeking opportunities to help diffuse that competence more broadly through the company.

Whether you lead from the top of your company or from an operating level, your effectiveness depends on a deep understanding of the leadership and political dynamics of your firm. Many senior executives develop this level of insight in the course of their career advancement. But if you happen to be new to the firm, you will need to do a little local research. Your goal is to identify the most receptive channels for implementing significant changes in how the firm makes important decisions. You will also need to know which people and channels will be most resistant. These activities are not without some jeopardy. Therefore, you must learn who among your peers and superiors will welcome change and who will resist—perhaps to the point of firing you for stepping too far out of line. Of course, you will more likely avoid career damage if you are effective and thorough in discussing, taking action, and leveraging early successes as a platform from which to diffuse change.

Concluding Thoughts

We'll repeat our core message: *firms that select the right ways to obtain new resources gain competitive advantages.* Selection capability is a discipline that you must nurture and develop over time. There are no easy fixes to selection problems. As stressed throughout this book, you cannot overcome selection mistakes by simply working harder to implement imperfect ways of sourcing resources.

The lack of a strong selection capability creates critical problems for any firm. Executives from established companies have repeatedly made this point to us after their firms—once industry leaders—became stuck in selection ruts or implementation traps and failed to successfully innovate. And young firms, racing to secure a market foothold, often neglect to consider a wide enough set of build-borrow-buy options. Instead, they struggle to advance beyond their start-up innovations.

The past can be a deadly rear-view mirror. To remedy competitive problems, firms often escalate their commitment to familiar growth paths and work harder to implement their projects. When that doesn't work, what comes next? Lacking an organized selection process, they might delegate a few executives or an ad hoc task force to identify and choose new sourcing opportunities. But even the smartest task force needs an orderly lens through which to evaluate the sourcing options.

The resource pathways framework is a powerful tool for any firm in any industry and any part of the world. It can prescribe the most effective ways of gathering key resources quickly and efficiently, allowing you to grow your business in the face of heated competition. As part of your strategic toolkit, the framework will generate advantages over rival firms that succumb to the implementation trap (see the full model of the framework in appendix A).

Finally, you need leadership—leadership for those who select each sourcing mode; those who lead internal development, M&A, contracts, and partnerships; those involved in coordinating and assuring the transparency of all sourcing activity; and the CEO and executive board, acting as high-level champions and authorizers of an enterprise build-borrow-buy discipline. Without leadership at all those levels, the initiative will founder.

Like any methodology, the resource pathways framework can be used carelessly, misinterpreted, or put to work inappropriately. If so, your selection capability will spin its wheels and lead to chaos rather than competence. As a leader, therefore, you must understand the context. Is there a business problem for which the framework is an indispensable missing piece? Is the organization ready to develop a strong selection capability? Can you identify the key enablers of enterprise change and find the best way to enlist their support?

If you can answer yes to those questions, you will foster and sustain vibrant new strategic opportunities for your business—and forge a successful career for yourself.

The Resource Pathways Framework: Full Model

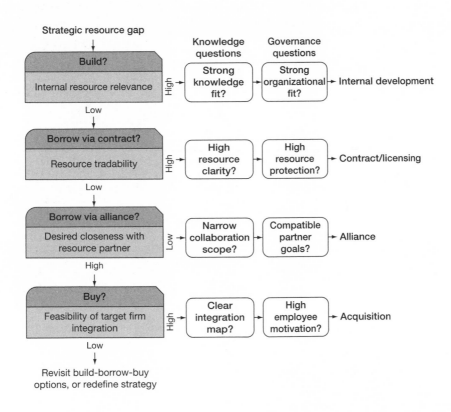

The Authors' Research Program

This book draws from two decades of our wide-ranging research and experience, and from studies by many other scholars in our field. The ideas and data we present here stem from multiple large-scale empirical studies and many interviews with senior executives across industries as diverse as auto manufacturing, life sciences, aerospace, consumer packaged goods, and telecommunications. Our research included the following studies:

- A structured survey of 162 telecom companies, worldwide, about their use of sourcing modes to close resource gaps, with follow-up survival analysis of the surveyed telecom companies

- A structured survey of 253 US and European acquisitions in manufacturing industries to assess the effectiveness of postmerger resource divestiture and redeployment during the early 1990s

- Longitudinal studies of several hundred pharmaceutical, medical-device, and health-services firms in the global life-sciences sector, encompassing data from the 1950s through the 2000s

- Analysis of panel data concerning business change during the 1990s and 2000s affecting several hundred firms based in East Asia

- Analysis of data ranging from a few dozen cases to several hundred companies in the global auto OEM and supplier sectors, online commerce, the aerospace industry, industrial manufacturing sector, and the banking industry

The results of these studies have shaped the ideas in the resource pathways framework. We have used these ideas in our classes for the past decade and more, benefiting as our students pushed us to develop and refine these concepts further. Most generally, we also draw on a wide array of strategy, economic, and organizational research by various other scholars.

If you wish to deepen your understanding of the issues in this book, we encourage you to select from the following readings those that fit your needs. The following list identifies some of our own studies that helped shape our thinking. We deeply appreciate and respect the depth and breadth of research that other scholars have generated in these fields; their work has provided the building blocks for our research and thinking and is listed in the book's References section.

Managerial Readings

Overview of the Resource Pathways Model

Capron, Laurence, and Will Mitchell. "Finding the Right Path." *Harvard Business Review,* July–August 2010, 102–107.

Capron, Laurence, Will Mitchell, and Joanne Oxley. "Organizing for Learning." *Financial Times* Mastering Strategy Series, November 29, 1999.

Managing Alliances

Mitchell, Will. "Alliances: Achieving Long-Term Value and Short-Term Goals," *Financial Times Mastering Strategy: The Complete MBA Companion in Strategy* (London: Pearson Education Limited, 2000), 351–356.

Dussauge, Pierre, Bernard Garrette, and Will Mitchell. "How to Get the Best Results from Alliances." *European Business Forum* 3, Fall 2000: 41–46.

Managing M&A

Mitchell, Will, and Laurence Capron. "Managing Acquisitions to Change and Survive." *European Business Forum* 9, Spring (2002): 51–55.

Capron, Laurence, and Kevin Kaiser. "Does Your M&A Add Value?" *Financial Times Managing in a Downturn,* February 6, 2009.

Capron, Laurence. "The Private M&A: Does the 'Private Firm' Discount Exist?" *Chief Executive,* October 8, 2008.

Capron, Laurence, and Mauro Guillén. "Fighting Economic Nationalism in M&As." *Financial Times* Mastering Strategy Series, October 13, 2006.

Capron, Laurence, and Karen Schnatterly. "How M&As Can Lead to Governance Failure." *Financial Times* Mastering Corporate Governance Series, June 3, 2005.

Capron, Laurence. "Horizontal Acquisitions: The Benefits and Risk to Long-Term Performance." *Financial Times* Mastering Strategy Series, November 8, 1999.

Managing Corporate Development

Karim, Samina, and Will Mitchell. "Innovation Through Acquisition and Internal Development: A Quarter-Century of Business Reconfiguration at Johnson & Johnson." *Long Range Planning* 37, no. 6 (2004): 525–547.

Case Studies

Capron, Laurence, Urs Peyer, and Lori Einheiber. "The Bid for Bell Canada Enterprises." Fontainebleau: INSEAD, 2011. (strategic versus financial buyer; LBO)

Hunter, Mark, Laurence Capron, and Fares Boulos. "Lloyds-TSB Group: Business Portfolio Restructuring and Development." Fontainebleau: INSEAD, 2011. (portfolio restructuring; role of corporate parent)

Garrette, Bernard, and Laurence Capron. "The Matra-Renault Alliance (A): Gearing Up to the 2002 Milestone." Jouy-en-Josas, France: HEC-INSEAD, 2010. (alliance management)

Garrette, Bernard, and Laurence Capron. "The Matra-Renault Alliance (B): Is There a Life after the Espace?" Jouy-en-Josas, France: HEC-INSEAD, 2010. (alliance management)

Capron, Laurence, and Nir Brueller. "Cisco Systems: New Millennium–New Acquisition Strategy?" Fountainebleau, France: INSEAD, 2010. (M&A integration)

Capron, Laurence, and Andrew Horncastle. "Acquisition Wave in the Fine Chemicals Industry (A): Clariant-BTP Acquisition." Fountainebleau, France: INSEAD, 2006. (M&A wave and industry fads)

Capron, Laurence, and Andrew Horncastle. "Acquisition Wave in the Fine Chemicals Industry (B): Rhodia-Chirex Acquisition." Fountainebleau, France: INSEAD, 2006. (M&A wave and industry fads)

Capron, Laurence, and Andrew Horncastle. "Acquisition Wave in the Fine Chemicals Industry (C): Degussa-Laporte." Fountainebleau, France: INSEAD, 2006. (M&A wave and industry fads)

Mitchell, Will. "Change Strategy at General Electric, 1980–2006." Durham, NC: Duke University, 2008. (multi-modal change)

Mitchell, Will. "Abbott International: Launching Kaletra in China in 2003." Durham, NC: Duke University, 2007. (internal development in non-traditional markets)

Mitchell, Will. "The CKD Clinic Proposal in Newark in 2003." Durham, NC: Duke University, 2007. (internal development)

Mitchell, Will. "Takeda Abbott Pharmaceuticals (TAP) in 2002." Durham, NC: Duke University, 2007. (alliances)

Santo-Rivera, Miguel, Pierre Dussauge, and Will Mitchell. "The Amazon–Toys"R"Us Alliance, 2000." Jouy-en-Josas, France: HEC-INSEAD, 2007. (alliances)

Mitchell, Will. "Pharmaceutical Introduction: Launching Eli Lilly's Sarafem in 2000 (A & B)." Durham, NC: Duke University, 2003. (internal development)

Mitchell, Will. "The Evolution of Astra Merck Inc., 1982–1999." Ann Arbor, MI: University of Michigan at Ann Arbor, 1998/2007. (alliances)

Mitchell, Will. "United States Office Products in 1998." Ann Arbor, MI: University of Michigan at Ann Arbor, 1998. (acquisitions)

Mitchell, Will. "Comparing Two Acquisitions: Marion Merrell Dow (1989) and Glaxo Wellcome (1995)." Durham, NC: Duke University, 2009. (acquisitions)

Mitchell, Will. "Playing Leapfrog with Elephants: EMI, Ltd. and CT Scanner Competition in the 1970s." Ann Arbor, MI: University of Michigan at Ann Arbor, 1997/2005. (industry life cycles)

Mitchell, Will. "Remora Among the Sharks: Imatron, Inc. and CT Scanner Competition in the 1980s." Ann Arbor, MI: University of Michigan at Ann Arbor, 1997. (industry life cycles)

Academic Readings

Selection Capability: Choosing Between Internal Development and External Sourcing

Capron, Laurence, and Will Mitchell. "Selection Capability: How Capability Gaps and Internal Social Frictions Affect Internal and External Strategic Renewal." *Organization Science* 20, no. 2 (2009): 294–312.

Capron, Laurence, and Will Mitchell. "Where Firms Change: Internal Development Versus External Capability Sourcing in the Global Telecommunications Industry." *European Management Review* 1, no. 2 (2004): 157–174.

Managing Internal Development

Mukherjee, Ashok, Brian Talbot, and Will Mitchell. "The Impact of New Manufacturing Requirements on Production Line Productivity and Quality at a Focused Factory." *Journal of Operations Management* 18, no. 2 (2000): 139–168.

Managing Contracts

Mulotte, Louis, Pierre Dussauge, and Will Mitchell. "Does Collaboration Induce Spurious Learning and Overconfidence? Evidence from Independent versus Collaborative Entry in the Global Aerospace Industry, 1944–2000." *Strategic Management Journal,* forthcoming 2012.

Parmigiani, Anne, and Will Mitchell. "The Hollow Corporation Revisited: Can Governance Mechanisms Substitute for Technical Expertise in Managing Buyer-Supplier Relationships?" *European Management Review* 7, no. 1 (2010): 46–70.

Managing Alliances

Singh, Kulwant, and Will Mitchell. "Growth Dynamics: The Bi-Directional Relationship between Interfirm Collaboration and Business Sales in Entrant and Incumbent Alliances." *Strategic Management Journal* 26 (2005): 497–522.

Singh, Kulwant, and Will Mitchell. "Precarious Collaboration: Business Survival after Partners Shut Down or Form New Partnerships." Special issue, *Strategic Management Journal* 17, no. 1 (1996): 99–115.

Mitchell, Will, Pierre Dussauge, and Bernard Garrette. "Alliances with Competitors: How to Combine and Protect Key Resources." Special issue, *Journal of Creativity and Innovation Management* 11, no. 3 (2002): 202–223.

Dussauge, Pierre, Bernard Garrette, and Will Mitchell. "Learning from Competing Partners: Outcomes and Durations of Scale and Link Alliances in Europe, North America, and Asia." *Strategic Management Journal* 21, no. 2 (2000): 99–126.

M&A, Value Creation, and Stock Returns

Capron, Laurence. "The Long-Term Performance of Horizontal Acquisitions." *Strategic Management Journal* 20, no. 11 (1999): 987–1018.

Capron, Laurence, and Jung-Chin Shen. "Acquisitions of Private versus Public Firms: Private Information, Target Selection and Acquirer Returns." *Strategic Management Journal* 28, no. 9 (2007): 891–911.

Capron, Laurence, and Nathalie Pistre. "When Do Acquirers Earn Abnormal Returns?" *Strategic Management Journal* 23, no. 9 (2002): 781–794.

Mitchell, Will, and Annetta Fortune. 2012. "Unpacking the Firm Exit at the Firm and Industry Levels: The Adaptation and Selection of Firm Capabilities." *Strategic Management Journal,* forthcoming 2012.

Managing Post-Merger Integration and Divestiture

Capron, Laurence, Pierre Dussauge, and Will Mitchell. "Resource Redeployment Following Horizontal Mergers and Acquisitions in Europe and North America, 1988–1992." *Strategic Management Journal* 19, no. 7 (1998): 631–661.

Capron, Laurence, Anand Swaminathan, and Will Mitchell. "Asset Divestiture Following Horizontal Acquisitions: A Dynamic View." *Strategic Management Journal* 22, no. 9 (2001): 817–844.

Capron, Laurence, and Will Mitchell. "Bilateral Resource Redeployment and Capabilities Improvement Following Horizontal Acquisitions." *Industrial and Corporate Change* 7, no. 3 (1998): 453–484.

Capron, Laurence, and Will Mitchell. "The Role of Acquisitions in Reshaping Business Capabilities in the International Telecommunications Industry." Special issue, *Industry and Corporate Change* 7, no. 4 (1998): 715–730.

Karim, Samina, and Will Mitchell. "Path-Dependent and Path-Breaking Change: Reconfiguring Business Resources Following Acquisitions in the U.S. Medical Sector, 1978–1995." Special issue, *Strategic Management Journal* 21, no. 10–11 (2000): 1061–1081.

Role of Institutional Environment on M&A and Other Growth Paths

Capron, Laurence, and Mauro Guillén. "National Corporate Governance Institutions and Post-Acquisition Target Reorganization." *Strategic Management Journal* 30, no. 8 (2009): 803–833.

Chakrabarti, Abhirup, Elena Vidal, and Will Mitchell. "Business Transformation in Heterogeneous Environments: The Impact of Market Development and Firm Strength on Growth and Retrenchment Reconfiguration." *Global Strategy Journal* 1, no. 1 (2011): 6–26.

References

Chapter 1

Amit, R., and Schoemaker, P. "Strategic Assets and Organizational Rent." *Strategic Management Journal* 14, no. 1 (1993): 33–46.

Barney, J. "Firm Resources and Sustained Competitive Advantage." *Journal of Management* 17, no. 1 (1991): 99–120.

Carroll, G. R., and M. T. Hannan (eds.). *Organizations in Industry: Strategy, Structure, and Selection.* New York: Oxford University Press, 1995.

Cohen, W. M., and D. Levinthal. "Absorptive Capacity: A New Perspective on Learning and Innovation." *Administrative Science Quarterly* 35, no. 1 (1990): 128–152.

Cusumano. M. A. *Staying Power: Six Enduring Principles for Managing Strategy and Innovation in an Uncertain World.* New York: Oxford University Press, 2010.

Cyert, R. M., and J. G. March. *A Behavioral Theory of the Firm.* Englewood Cliffs, NJ: Prentice-Hall, 1963.

De Wit, F. R. C., L. L. Greer, and K. A. Jehn. "The Paradox of Intragroup Conflict: A Meta-Analysis." *Journal of Applied Psychology* 97, no. 2 (2012): 360–390.

Dosi, G. "Technological Paradigms and Technological Trajectories." *Research Policy* 11, no. 3 (1982): 147–162.

Eisenhardt, K. M., and J. A. Martin. "Dynamic Capabilities: What Are They?" *Strategic Management Journal* 21 (2000): 1105–1121.

Galunic, D. C., and S. Rodan. "Resource Recombinations in the Firm: Knowledge Structures and the Potential for Schumpetarian Recombination." *Strategic Management Journal* 19, no. 12 (1998): 1193–1201.

Hannan, M. T., and J. Freeman. "Structural Inertia and Organizational Change." *American Sociological Review* 49, no. 2 (1984): 149–164.

Helfat, C. E., S. Finkelstein, W. Mitchell, M. A. Peteraf, H. Singh, D. J. Teece, and S. G. Winter. *Dynamic Capabilities: Understanding Strategic Change in Organizations.* Malden, MA: Blackwell, 2007.

Kaplan, S. "Cognition, Capabilities, and Incentives: Assessing Firm Response to the Fiber-Optic Revolution." *Academy of Management Journal* 51, no. 4 (2008): 672–695.

Kriauciunas, A., and P. Kale. "The Impact of Environmental Imprinting and Search on Resource Change: A Study of Firms in Lithuania." *Strategic Management Journal* 27, no. 7 (2006): 659–679.

Leonard, D. *Wellsprings of Knowledge: Building and Sustaining the Sources of Innovation.* Boston: Harvard Business School Press, 1995.

Levinthal, D. "Organizational Adaptation and Environmental Selection: Interrelated Processes of Change." *Organization Science* 2, no. 1 (1991): 140–146.

Liebeskind, J. P. "Knowledge, Strategy, and the Theory of the Firm." *Strategic Management Journal* 17, Winter (1996): 93–107.

Mahoney, J. T., and J. R. Pandian. "The Resource-Based View Within the Conversation of Strategic Management." *Strategic Management Journal* 13, no. 5 (1992): 363–380.

Nelson, R. R., and S. G. Winter. *An Evolutionary Theory of Economic Change*. Cambridge, MA: Belknap Press of Harvard University Press, 1982.

Penrose, E. T. *The Theory of the Growth of the Firm*. New York: John Wiley, 1959.

Pisano, G. "The R&D Boundaries of the Firm: An Empirical Analysis." *Administrative Science Quarterly* 35, no. 1 (1990): 153–176.

Schumpeter, J. A. *The Theory of Economic Development: An Inquiry into Profits, Capital, Credit, Interest, and the Business Cycle*. Cambridge, MA: Harvard University Press, 1934.

Teece, D. J., G. Pisano, and A. Shuen. "Dynamic Capabilities and Strategic Management." *Strategic Management Journal* 18, no. 7 (1997): 509–533.

Tripsas, M., and G. Gavetti. "Capabilities, Cognition, and Inertia: Evidence from Digital Imaging." *Strategic Management Journal* 21, no. 10–11 (2000): 1147–1161.

Tushman, M. L., and C. A. O'Reilly. "The Ambidextrous Organization: Managing Evolutionary and Revolutionary Change." *California Management Review* 38, no. 4 (1996): 8–30.

Tushman, M. L., and P. Anderson. "Technological Discontinuities and Organizational Environments." *Administrative Science Quarterly* 31, no. 3 (1986): 439–465.

Winter, S. "Survival, Selection, and Inheritance in Evolutionary Theories of Evolution." In *Organizational Evolution: New Directions*, edited by J. V. Singh, 269–296. Newbury Park, CA: Sage Publications, 1990.

Winter, S. G. "Understanding Dynamic Capabilities." *Strategic Management Journal* 24, no. 10 (2003): 991–995.

Zollo, M., and S. G. Winter. "Deliberate Learning and the Evolution of Dynamic Capabilities." *Organization Science* 13, no. 3 (2002): 339–351.

Chapter 2

Argote, L. *Organizational Learning: Creating, Retaining, and Transferring Knowledge*. Boston: Kluwer Academic, 1999.

Barnett, W. P., and G. R. Carroll. "Modeling Internal Organizational Change." In X. Hagan (ed.), *Annual Review of Sociology*, vol. 21 (1995): 217–236.

Barney, J. "How a Firm's Capabilities Affect Boundary Decisions." *Sloan Management Review* 40, no. 3 (1999): 137–145.

Burgelman, R. "Corporate Entrepreneurship and Strategic Management: Insights from a Process Study." *Management Science* 29, no. 12 (1983): 1349–1364.

Chatterjee, S. "Excess Capabilities, Utilization Costs, and Mode of Entry." *Academy of Management Journal* 33, no. 4 (1990): 780–800.

Chesbrough, H. "The Governance and Performance of Xerox's Technology Spin-off Companies." *Research Policy* 32, no. 3 (2003): 403–421.

Christensen, C. M. *The Innovator's Dilemma: When New Technologies Cause Great Firms to Fail*. Boston: Harvard Business School Press, 1997.

Delmas, M. "Exposing Strategic Assets to Create New Competencies: The Case of Technological Acquisition in the Waste Management Industry in Europe and North America." *Industrial and Corporate Change* 8, no. 4 (1999): 635–671.

Dierickx, I., and K. Cool. "Asset Stock Accumulation and Sustainability of Competitive Advantage." *Management Science* 35, no. 12 (1989): 1504–1514.

Gawer, A., and R. Henderson. "Platform Owner Entry and Innovation in Complementary Markets: Evidence from Intel." *Journal of Economics & Management Strategy* 16, no.1 (2007): 1–34.

Hargadon, A., and R. I. Sutton. "Technology Brokering and Innovation in a Product Development Firm." *Administrative Science Quarterly* 42, no. 4 (1997): 716–749.

Helfat, C. E. "Evolutionary Trajectories in Petroleum Firm R&D." *Management Science* 40, no. 12 (1994): 1720–1747.

Helfat, C. E., and M. B. Lieberman. "The Birth of Capabilities: Market Entry and the Importance of Pre-History." *Industrial and Corporate Change* 11, no. 4 (2002): 725–760.

Helfat, C. E., and M. Peteraf. "The Dynamic-Resource-Based View: Capability Lifecycles." *Strategic Management Journal* 24, no. 10 (2003): 997–1010.

Henderson, R. M., and K. B. Clark. "Architectural Innovation: The Reconfiguration of Existing Product Technologies and the Failure of Established Firms." *Administrative Science Quarterly* 35, no. 1 (1990): 9–30.

Hennart, J. F., and Y. Park. "Greenfield vs. Acquisition: The Strategy of Japanese Investors in the United States." *Management Science* 39, no. 9 (1993): 1054–1070.

Jacobides, M., and S. Winter. "The Co-evolution of Capabilities and Transaction Costs: Explaining the Institutional Structure of Production." *Strategic Management Journal* 26, no. 5 (2005): 395–413.

Jacobides, M., and S. Billinger. "Designing the Boundaries of the Firm: From 'Make, Buy, or Ally' to the Dynamic Benefits of Vertical Architecture." *Organization Science* 17, no. 2 (2006): 249–261.

Katila, R., and A. Ahuja. "Something Old, Something New: A Longitudinal Study of Search Behavior and New Product Introduction." *Academy of Management Journal* 45, no. 6 (2002): 1183–1194.

Kogut, B., and U. Zander. "Knowledge of the Firm, Combinative Capabilities, and the Replication of Technology." *Organization Science* 3, no. 3 (1992): 383–397.

Kogut, B., and U. Zander. "What Firms Do? Coordination, Identity and Learning." *Organization Science* 7, no. 5 (1996): 502–518.

Lavie, D. "Capability Reconfiguration: An Analysis of Incumbent Responses to Technological Change." *Academy of Management Review* 31, no. 1 (2006): 153–174.

Markides, C. C., and P. J. Williamson. "Related Diversification, Core Competencies, and Corporate Performance." *Strategic Management Journal* 15, no. 2 (1994): 149–165.

Menon, T., and J. Pfeffer. "Valuing Internal vs. External Knowledge: Explaining the Preference for Outsiders." *Management Science* 49, no. 4 (2003): 497–514.

Palepu, K., and T. Khanna. "Why Focused Strategies May Be Wrong for Emerging Markets." *Harvard Business Review*, July–August 1997, 41–51.

Peteraf, M. A., "The Cornerstones of Competitive Advantage: A Resource-Based View." *Strategic Management Journal* 14, no. 3 (1993): 179–191.

Raisch, S., J. M. Birkinshaw, G. Probst, and M. Tushman. "Organizational Ambidexterity: Balancing Exploration for Sustained Corporate Performance." *Organization Science* 20, no. 4 (2009): 685–695.

Rosenkopf, L., and A. Nerkar. "Beyond Local Search: Boundary-Spanning, Exploration, and Impact in the Optical Disc Industry." *Strategic Management Journal* 22, no. 4 (2001): 287–306.

Santos, F. M., and K. K. Eisenhardt. "Organizational Boundaries and Theories of Organization." *Organization Science* 16, no. 5 (2005): 491–508.

Shaver, J. M. "Accounting for Endogeneity When Assessing Strategy Performance: Does Entry Mode Choice Affect FDI Survival?" *Management Science* 44, no. 4 (1998): 571–585.

Siggelkow, N. "Change in the Presence of Fit: The Rise, the Fall, and the Renaissance of Liz Claiborne." *Academy of Management Journal* 44, no. 4 (2001): 838–858.

Silverman, B. "Technological Resources and the Direction of Corporate Diversification: Toward an Integration of the Resource-Based View and Transaction Cost Economics." *Management Science* 45, no. 8 (1999): 1109–1124.

Stuart, T. E., and J. M. Podolny. "Local Search and the Evolution of Technological Capabilities." *Strategic Management Journal* 17, Evolutionary Perspectives on Strategy Supplement (1996): 21–38.

Szulanski, G. "Exploring Internal Stickiness: Impediments to the Transfer of the Best Practice Within the Firm." *Strategic Management Journal* 17, Winter Special Issue (1996): 27–44.

Von Hippel, E. "Innovation by User Communities: Learning from Open-Source Software." *MIT Sloan Management Review* 42, no. 4 (2001): 82.

Wernerfelt, B. "A Resource-Based View of the Firm." *Strategic Management Journal* 5, no. 2 (1984): 171–180.

White, S. "Competition, Capabilities, and the Make, Buy, or Ally Decisions of Chinese State-Owned Firms." *Academy of Management Journal* 43, no. 3 (2000): 324–341.

Yip, G. "Diversification Entry: Internal Development versus Acquisition." *Strategic Management Journal* 3, no. 4 (1982): 331–345.

Chapter 3

Anand, B., and T. Khanna. "The Structure of Licensing Contracts." *Journal of Industrial Economics* 48, no. 1 (2000): 103–135.

Argyres, N. S., and K. J. Mayer. "Contract Design as a Firm Capability: An Integration of Learning and Transaction Cost Perspectives." *Academy of Management Review* 32, no. 4 (2007): 1060–1077.

Arora, A., A. Fosfuri, and A. Gambardella. *Markets for Technology: The Economics of Innovation and Corporate Strategy.* Cambridge, MA: MIT Press, 2001.

Arora, A., A. Fosfuri, and A. Gambardella. "Markets for Technology and Corporate Strategy." *Industrial and Corporate Change* 10, no. 2 (2001): 419–451.

Arora, A., and A. Gambardella. "Complementary and External Linkages: The Strategies of the Large Firms in Biotechnology." *Journal of Industrial Economy* 3, no. 4 (1990): 361–379.

Barney, J. B. "Strategic Factor Markets: Expectations, Luck, and Business Strategy." *Management Science* 32, no. 10 (1986): 1231–1240.

Cassiman, B., and R. Veugelers. "In Search of Complementarity in Innovation Strategy: Internal R&D and External Knowledge Acquisition." *Management Science* 52, no. 1 (2006): 68–82.

Chi, T. "Trading in Strategic Capabilities: Necessary Conditions, Transaction Cost Problems, and Choice of Exchange Structure." *Strategic Management Journal* 15, no. 4 (1994): 271–290.

Gans, J. S., and S. Stern. "The Product Market and the Market for Ideas: Commercialization Strategies for Technology Entrepreneurs." *Research Policy* 32, no. 2 (2003): 333–350.

Kale, P., and P. Puranam. "Choosing Equity Stakes in Technology Sourcing Relationships: An Integrative Framework." *California Management Review* 46, Spring (2004): 77–99.

Mathews, J. "Strategizing by Firms in the Presence of Markets for Resources." *Industrial and Corporate Change* 12, no. 6 (2003): 1157–1193.

Mayer, K. J., and R. Salomon. "Capabilities, Contractual Hazard and Governance: Integrating Resource-Based and Transaction Cost Perspectives." *Academy of Management Journal* 49, no. 5 (2006): 942–959.

Teece, D. J. "Profiting from Technological Innovation: Implications for Integration, Collaboration, and Public Policy." *Research Policy* 15, no. 6 (1986): 285–305.

Van de Vrande, V., C. Lemmens, and W. Vanhaverbeke. "Choosing Governance Modes for External Technology Sourcing." *R&D Management* 36, no. 3 (2006): 347–363.

Vanneste, B. S., and P. Puranam. "Repeated Interactions and Contractual Detail: Identifying the Learning Effect." *Organization Science* 21, no. 1 (2010): 186–201.

Williamson, O. E. *Markets and Hierarchies, Analysis and Antitrust Implications: A Study in the Economics of Internal Organization*. New York: Free Press, 1975.

Williamson, O. E. *The Economic Institutions of Capitalism: Firms, Markets, Relational Contracting*. New York: Free Press, 1985.

Ziedonis, R. "Don't Fence Me In: Fragmented Markets for Technology and the Patent Acquisition Strategies of Firms." *Management Science* 50, no. 6 (2004): 804–820.

Chapter 4

Anderson, E., and H. Gatignon. "Models of Foreign Entry: A Transaction Cost Analysis and Propositions." *Journal of International Business Studies* 17, no. 3 (1986): 1–26.

Balakrishnan, S., and M. P. Koza. "Information Asymmetry, Adverse Selection and Joint Ventures." *Journal of Economic Behavior and Organization* 20, no. 1 (1993): 99–117.

David, J. P., and K. M. Eisenhardt. "Rotating Leadership and Collaborative Innovation: Recombination Processes in Symbiotic Relationships." *Administrative Science Quarterly* 56, no. 2 (2011): 159–201.

Doz, Y. "The Evolution of Cooperation in Strategic Alliances: Initial Conditions, or Learning Processes?" *Strategic Management Journal* 17, Summer (1996): 175–183.

Doz, Y., and G. Hamel. *Alliance Advantage: The Art of Creating Value through Partnering*. Boston: Harvard Business School Press, 1998.

Dussauge, P., and B. Garrette. *Cooperative Strategy: Competing Successfully Through Strategic Alliances*. New York: John Wiley, 1999.

Dyer, J. H., P. Kale, and H. Singh. "When to Ally and When to Acquire." *Harvard Business Review*, July–August 2004, 109–115.

Dyer, J. H., and H. Singh. "The Relational View: Cooperative Strategy and Sources of Interorganizational Competitive Advantage." *Academy of Management Review* 23, no. 4 (1998): 660–674.

Folta, T. B. "Governance and Uncertainty: The Tradeoff Between Administrative Control and Commitment." *Strategic Management Journal* 19, no. 11 (1998): 1007–1028.

Garrette, B., and P. Dussauge. "Alliances versus Acquisitions: Choosing the Right Option." *European Management Journal* 18, no. 1 (2000): 63–69.

Garrette, B., X. Castañer, and P. Dussauge. "Horizontal Alliances as an Alternative to Autonomous Production: Product Expansion Mode Choice in the Worldwide Aircraft Industry 1945–2000." *Strategic Management Journal* 30, no. 8 (2009): 885–894.

Gulati, R., and H. Singh. "The Architecture of Cooperation: Managing Coordination Costs and Appropriation Concerns in Strategic Alliances." *Administrative Science Quarterly* 43, no. 4 (1998): 781–814.

Hamel, G. "Competition for Competence and Inter-Partner Learning Within International Strategic Alliances." *Strategic Managment Journal* 12, no. 1 (1991): 83–103.

Hennart, J.-F. "A Transaction Costs Theory of Equity Joint Ventures." *Strategic Management Journal* 9, no. 4 (1988): 361.

Inkpen, A. C., and P. W. Beamish. "Knowledge, Bargaining Power, and the Instability of International Joint Ventures." *Academy of Management Review* 22, no. 1 (1997): 177–202.

Kale, P., and J. Anand. "The Decline of Emerging Economy Joint Ventures: The Case of India." *California Management Review* 48, no. 3 (2006): 61–76.

Kale, P., J. H. Dyer, and H. Singh. "Alliance Capability, Stock Market Response, and Long-term Alliance Success: The Role of the Alliance Function." *Strategic Management Journal* 23, no. 8 (2002): 747–767.

Kale, P., and M. Zollo. "Understanding Partnering Processes and Outcomes: The Contribution of Evolutionary Theory." In *Handbook of Strategic Alliances*, edited by O. Shenkar and J. J. Reuer, 81–99. London: Sage Publications, 2005.

Khanna, T., R. Gulati, and N. Nohria. "The Dynamics of Learning Alliances: Competition, Cooperation, and Relative Scope." *Strategic Management Journal* 19, no. 3 (1998): 193–210.

Kogut, B. "Joint Ventures: Theoretical and Empirical Perspectives." *Strategic Management Journal* 9, no. 4 (1988): 319–332.

Kogut, B. "Joint Ventures and the Option to Expand and Acquire." *Management Science* 37, no. 1 (1991): 19–33.

Lavid, D., and L. Rosenkopf. "Balancing Exploration and Exploitation in Alliance Formation." *Academy of Management Journal* 49, no. 4 (2006): 797–818.

Mesquita, L. F., J. Anand, and T. H. Brush. "Comparing the Resource-Based and Relational Views: Knowledge Transfer and Spillover in Vertical Alliances." *Strategic Management Journal* 29, no. 9 (2008): 913–941.

Mowery, D., J. Oxley, and B. Silverman. "Strategic Alliances and Interfirm Knowledge Transfer." *Strategic Management Journal* 17, Winter Special Issue (1996): 77–91.

Oxley, J. E. "Institutional Environment and the Mechanisms of Governance: The Impact of Intellectual Property Protection on the Structure of Inter-Firm Alliances." *Journal of Economic Behavior and Organization* 38, no. 3 (1999): 283–309.

Oxley, J. E., and R.C. Sampson. "The Scope and Governance of International R&D Alliances." *Strategic Management Journal* 25, no. 8–9 (2004): 723–749.

Reuer, J., and A. Arino. "Strategic Alliance Contracts: Dimensions and Determinants of Contractual Complexity." *Strategic Management Journal* 28, no. 3 (2007): 313–330.

Reuer, J., and M. P. Koza. "On Lemons and Indigestibility: Resource Assembly Through Joint Ventures." *Strategic Management Journal* 21, no. 2 (2000): 195–197.

Rosenkopf, L., and P. Almeida. "Overcoming Local Search Through Alliances and Mobility." *Management Science* 49, no. 6 (2003): 751–766.

Rothaermel, F. "Incumbent's Advantage Through Exploiting Complementary Assets via Interfirm Cooperation." *Strategic Management Journal* 22, no. 6–7 (2001): 687–699.

Simonin, B. L. "The Importance of Collaborative Know-how: An Empirical Test of the Learning Organization." *Academy of Management Journal* 40, no. 5 (1997): 1150–1174.

Singh, Kulwant. "The Impact of Technological Complexity and Interfirm Cooperation on Firm Survival." *Academy of Management Journal* 40, no. 2 (1997): 339–367.

Vanhaverbeke, W., G. Duysters, and N. Noorderhaven. "External Technology Sourcing Through Alliances or Acquisitions: An Analysis of the Application-Specific Integrated Circuits Industry." *Organization Science* 13, no. 6 (2002): 714.

Wang, L., and E. Zajac. "Alliance or Acquisition? A Dyadic Perspective on Interfirm Resource Combinations." *Strategic Management Journal* 28, no. 13 (2007): 89–105.

Chapter 5

Ahuja, G., and R. Katila. "Technological Acquisitions and the Innovation Performance of Acquiring Firms: A Longitudinal Study." *Strategic Management Journal* 22, no. 3 (2001): 197–220.

Anand, J., and A. Delios. "Absolute and Relative Resources as Determinants of International Acquisitions." *Strategic Management Journal* 23, no. 2 (2002): 119–134.

Anand J., and H. Singh. "Asset Redeployment, Acquisitions, and Corporate Strategy in Declining Industries." *Strategic Management Journal* 18, no. 1 (1997): 99–118.

Barkema, H. G., and M. Schijven. "How Do Firms Learn to Make Acquisitions? A Review of Past Research and an Agenda for the Future." *Journal of Management* 34, no. 3 (2008): 594–634.

Barkema, H. G., and M. Schijven. "Toward Unlocking the Full Potential of Acquisitions: The Role of Organizational Restructuring." *Academy of Management Journal* 51, no. 4 (2008): 696–722.

Birkinshaw, J. "Acquiring Intellect: Managing the Integration of Knowledge-Intensive Acquisitions." *Business Horizons*, May 1999, 33–40.

Brannen, M. Y., and M. F. Peterson. "Merging Without Alienating: Interventions Promoting Cross-Cultural Organizational Integration and Their Limitations." *Journal of International Business Study* 40, no. 3 (2009): 468–489.

Buono, A. F., and J. L. Bodwitch. *The Human Side of Mergers and Acquisitions: Managing Collisions Between People, Cultures, and Organizations.* San Francisco: Jossey-Bass, 1989.

Chaudhuri, S., and B. Tabrizi. "Capturing the Real Value in High-Tech Acquisitions." *Harvard Business Review*, September–October 1999, 123–130.

Coff, R. "Bidding Wars over R&D Intensive Firms: Knowledge, Opportunism, and the Market for Corporate Control." *Academy of Management Journal* 46, no. 1 (2003): 74–85.

Graebner, M. E., and M. K. Eisenhardt. "The Seller's Side of the Story: Acquisition as Courtship and Governance as Syndicate in Entrepreneurial Firms." *Administrative Science Quarterly* 49, no. 3 (2004): 366–403.

Graebner, M. E., M. K. Eisenhardt, and F. T. Roundy. "Success and Failure in Technology Acquisitions: Lessons for Buyers and Sellers." *The Academy of Management Perspectives* 24, no. 3 (2010): 73–92.

Haleblian, J., and S. Finkelstein. "The Influence of Organizational Acquisition Experience on Acquisition Performance: A Behavioral Learning Perspective." *Administrative Science Quarterly* 44, no. 1 (1999): 29–56.

Haspeslagh, P. C., and D. B. Jemison. *Managing Acquisitions: Creating Value Through Corporate Renewal.* New York: Free Press, 1991.

Haunschild, P. R., A. Davis-Blake, and M. Fichman. "Managerial Overcommitment in Corporate Acquisition Processes." *Organization Science* 5, no. 4 (1994): 528–540.

Hayward, M. L. A. "Professional Influence: The Effects of Investment Banks on Clients' Acquisition Financing and Performance." *Strategic Management Journal* 24, no. 9 (2003): 783–801.

Hayward, M. L. A., and D. C. Hambrick. "Explaining the Premium Paid for Larger Acquisitions: Evidence of CEO Hubris." *Administrative Science Quarterly* 42, no. 1 (1997): 103–127.

Jensen, M. C. "Agency Costs of Free Cash Flow, Corporate Finance, and Takeovers." *American Economic Review* 76, no. 2 (1986): 323–329.

Karim, S. "Modularity in Organizational Structure: The Reconfiguration of Internally Developed and Acquired Business Units." *Strategic Management Journal* 27, no. 9 (2006): 799–823.

Larsson R., and S. Finkelstein. "Integrating Strategic, Organizational, and Human Resource Perspectives on Mergers and Acquisitions: A Case Survey of Synergy Realization." *Organization Science* 10, no. 1 (1999): 1–26.

Lee, G. K., and M. B. Lieberman. "Acquisitions vs. Internal Development as Modes of Market Entry." *Strategic Management Journal* 31, no. 2 (2010): 140–158.

Lubatkin, M. "Merger Strategy and Stockholder Value." *Strategic Management Journal* 8, no. 1 (1987): 39–54.

Marks, M. L., and P. H. Mirvis. "Making Mergers and Acquisitions Work: Strategic and Psychological Preparation." *Academy of Management Executive* 15, no. 2 (2001): 80–92.

Pangarkar, N., and J. R. Lie. "The Impact of Market Cycle on the Performance of the Singapore Acquirers." *Strategic Management Journal* 25, no. 12 (2004):1209–1216.

Puranam, P., H. Singh, and M. Zollo. "Organizing for Innovation: Managing the Autonomy Dilemma in Technology Acquisitions." *Academy of Management Journal* 49, no. 2 (2006): 263–280.

Puranam, P., and K. Srikanth. "What They Know versus What They Do: How Acquirers Leverage Technology Acquisitions." *Strategic Management Journal* 28, no. 8 (2007): 805–825.

Ranft, A. L., and M. D. Lord. "Acquiring New Technologies and Capabilities: A Grounded Model of Acquisition Implementation." *Organization Science* 13, no. 4 (2002): 420–441.

Schneper, W. D., and M. F. Guillén. "Stakeholder Rights and Corporate Governance: A Cross-National Study of Hostile Takeovers." *Administrative Science Quarterly* 49, no. 2 (2004): 263–295.

Seth, A. "Value Creation in Acquisitions: A Reexamination of Performance Issues." *Strategic Management Journal* 11, no. 2 (1990): 99–115.

Vermeulen, F., and H. Barkema. "Learning Through Acquisitions." *Academy of Management Journal* 44, no. 3 (2001): 457–476.

Zollo, M., and H. Singh. "Deliberate Learning in Corporate Acquisitions: Post-Acquisition Strategies and Integration Capability in U.S. Bank Mergers." *Strategic Management Journal* 25, no. 12 (2004): 1233–1256.

Chapter 6

Agarwal, R., R. Echambadi, A. Franco, and M. B. Sarkar. "Knowledge Transfer Through Inheritance: Spin-out Generation, Growth and Survival." *Academy of Management Journal* 47, no. 4 (2004): 501–522.

Bergh, D., R. Johnson, and R. Dewitt. "Restructuring Through Spin-off or Sell-off: Transforming Information Asymmetries into Financial Gain." *Strategic Management Journal* 29, no. 2 (2008): 133–148.

Berry, H. "Why Do Firms Divest?" *Organization Science* 21, no. 2 (2009): 380–398.

Burgelman, R. "Fading Memories: A Process Theory of Strategic Business Exit in Dynamic Environments." *Administrative Science Quarterly* 39, no. 1 (1994): 24–56.

Chang, S. J. "An Evolutionary Perspective on Diversification and Corporate Restructuring: Entry, Exit, and Economic Performance During 1981–89." *Strategic Management Journal* 17, no. 8 (1996): 587–611.

Helfat, C. E., and Peteraf, M. A. "The Dynamic-Resource-Based View: Capability Life-cycles." *Strategic Management Journal* 24, no. 10 (2003): 997–1010.

Helfat, C. E., and K. M. Eisenhardt. "Inter-Temporal Economies of Scope, Organizational Modularity, and the Dynamics of Diversification." *Strategic Management Journal* 25, no. 13 (2004): 1217–1232.

Hoetker, G., and R. Agarwal. "Death Hurts, but It Isn't Fatal: The Post-Exit Diffusion of Knowledge Created by Innovative Companies." *Academy of Management Journal* 50, no. 2 (2007): 446–467.

Kaul, A. "Technology and Corporate Scope: Firm and Rival Innovation as Antecedents of Corporate Transactions." *Strategic Management Journal* 33, no. 4 (2012): 347–367.

Kumar, S. "The Value from Acquiring and Divesting a Joint Venture: A Real Options Approach." *Strategic Management Journal* 26, no. 4 (2005): 321–331.

Levinthal, D., and B. Wu. "Opportunity Costs and Non-Scale Free Capabilities: Profit Maximization, Corporate Scope, and Profit Margins." *Strategic Management Journal* 31, no. 7 (2010): 780–801.

Markides, C. C. *Diversification, Refocusing, and Economic Performance.* Cambridge, MA: MIT Press, 1996.

McKendrick, D., J. Wade, and J. Jaffee. "A Good Riddance? Spin-offs and the Technological Performance of Parent Firms." *Organization Science* 20, no. 6 (2009): 979–992.

Moliterno, T. P., and M. F. Wiersema. "Firm Performance, Rent Appropriation, and the Strategic Resource Divestment Capability." *Strategic Management Journal* 28, no. 11 (2007): 1065–1087.

Montgomery, C. A., and A. R. Thomas. "Divestment: Motives and Gains." *Strategic Management Journal* 9, no. 1 (1988): 93–97.

Moschieri, C. "The Implementation and Structuring of Divestitures: The Unit's Perspective." *Strategic Management Journal* 32, no. 4 (2011): 368–401.

Moschieri, C., and J. Mair. "Research on Corporate Divestitures: A Synthesis." *Journal of Management & Organization* 14, no. 4 (2008): 399–422.

Penner-Hahn, J., and J. M. Shaver. "Does International Research and Development Increase Patent Output? An Analysis of Japanese Pharmaceutical Firms." *Strategic Management Journal* 26, no. 2 (2005): 121–140.

Reuer, R., and M. Zollo. "Termination Outcomes of Research Alliances." *Research Policy* 34, no. 1 (2005): 101–115.

Salomon, R., and X. Martin. "Learning, Knowledge Transfer, and Technology Implementation Performance: A Study of Time-to-Build in the Global Semiconductor Industry." *Management Science* 54, no. 7 (2008): 1266–1280.

Villalonga, B., and A. M. McGahan. "The Choice Among Acquisitions, Alliances, and Divestitures." *Strategic Management Journal* 26, no. 13 (2005): 1183–1208.

Zuckerman, E. "Focusing the Corporate Product: Securities Analysts and Dediversification." *Administrative Science Quarterly* 45, no. 3 (2000): 591–619.

Chapter 7

Arikan, A. M., and R. M. Stulz. "Corporate Acquisitions, Diversification, and the Firm's Lifecycle." Working paper 17463, National Bureau of Economic Research, 2011.

Barkema, H., and F. Vermeulen. "International Expansion Through Start-up or Acquisition: A Learning Perspective." *Academy of Management Journal* 41 (1998): 7–26.

Benson, D., and R. Ziedonis. "Corporate Venture Capital and the Returns to Acquiring Portfolio Companies." *Journal of Financial Economics* 8, no. 3 (2010): 478–499.

Chesbrough, H. *Open Innovation: The New Imperative for Creating and Profiting from Technology*. Boston: Harvard Business School Press, 2003.

Dowell, G. W. S., and A. Swaminathan. "Entry Timing, Exploration, and Firm Survival in the Early Years of the U.S. Bicycle Industry." *Strategic Management Journal* 27, no. 12 (2006): 1159–1182.

Dushnitsky, G., and M. J. Lenox. "When Do Incumbents Learn from Entrepreneurial Ventures? Corporate Venture Capital and Investing Firm Innovation Rates." *Research Policy* 34, no. 5 (2005): 615–639.

Kim, J.-Y., J. Haleblian, and S. Finkelstein. "When Firms Are Desperate to Grow via Acquisition: The Effect of Growth Patterns and Acquisition Experience on Acquisition Premiums." *Administrative Science Quarterly* 56, no. 3 (2011): 26–60.

Laamanen, T., and T. Keil. "Performance of Serial Acquirers: Toward an Acquisition Program Perspective." *Strategic Management Journal* 29, no. 6 (2008): 663–672.

Zollo, M., and J. Reuer. "Experience Spillover Across Corporate Development Activities." *Organization Science* 21, no. 6 (2010): 1195–1212.

Index

About the Authors

Laurence Capron is the Paul Desmarais Chaired Professor of Partnership and Active Ownership at INSEAD in France and Director of INSEAD's Executive Education Program on M&A and Corporate Strategy. Her teaching and research activities focus on M&A, alliances, corporate development, and portfolio strategy. She teaches in the MBA, executive MBA, executive education, and PhD programs at INSEAD. She is the author of numerous articles, including "Finding the Right Path" in *Harvard Business Review* (with Will Mitchell).

Laurence has received numerous professional honors and awards, including the INSEAD Best Teaching Award for her MBA elective, M&A and Corporate Strategy, which she has taught at INSEAD and Wharton. She is also the recipient of prestigious research awards, including the Academy of Management's Best Paper Award, McKinsey/Strategic Management Society Award, and HEC Paris Foundation Best Doctoral Dissertation Award. She won the 2011 Prix Académique Syntec du Conseil en Management in France for the best research paper in the strategy and finance category. Her current research focuses on how companies obtain new resources and use M&A, alliances, and licensing to supplement their organic growth.

Laurence joined INSEAD in 1997 after earning her PhD in strategy from HEC Paris. She was Visiting Professor of Strategy at MIT Sloan (2011–2012), Wharton (2005–2006), and Kellogg (2004–2005). From 2007 to 2010, she directed the INSEAD-Wharton Alliance. She sits on the editorial board of *Strategic Management Journal*.

Will Mitchell is the J. Rex Fuqua Professor of International Management at Duke University's Fuqua School of Business. Will also holds the Anthony S. Fell Chair in New Technologies and Commercialization at the University of Toronto, where he currently serves as a Visiting Professor of Strategic Management in the Rotman School of Management. Will earned a PhD degree at the School of Business Administration of the University of California at Berkeley and a BBA degree at Simon Fraser University in Vancouver. Before joining Duke University, he was a faculty member at the University of Michigan.

Will teaches in the MBA, PhD, and executive education programs at Duke and the University of Toronto, as well as in programs in Africa, Asia, and elsewhere. He teaches courses in business dynamics, emerging-market strategy, corporate strategy, entrepreneurship, health sector management, and pharmaceutical strategy.

Will studies business dynamics in developed and emerging markets, investigating how businesses change as their competitive environments change and, in turn, how these business changes contribute to ongoing corporate and social success or failure. The research emphasizes technical and organizational change, including information technology, product technology, organizational processes and structures, and institutional environments. He has published extensively in the strategy and medical services literatures. His current research focuses on how firms select and then manage different modes of change, such as mergers and acquisitions, alliances, discrete resource exchange, and internal development. He is studying the causes and effects of such changes for firms operating in several industrial sectors in North America, Europe, Asia, and Africa, with particular focus on life-sciences firms and numerous firms and groups that operate in emerging markets.

Will is active in professional and corporate organizations. He is a coeditor of *Strategic Management Journal*; an editorial board member on several strategy-related journals in North America, Asia, and Europe; and a board member of Neuland Laboratories, Ltd. (Hyderabad).